Addition & Subtraction

with Cuisenaire® Rods

Second Edition

by Patricia S. Davidson

by Patricia S. Davidson, Ed.D.

ETA hand2mind®

hands-on learning
for growing minds

Vernon Hills, IL

Written by: Patricia S. Davidson, Ed.D.

Addition & Subtraction with Cuisenaire® Rods
Second Edition

hand2mind 40715
ISBN 978-0-7406-0085-2

500 Greenview Court • Vernon Hills, IL 60061-1862 • 800.445.5985 • **hand2mind.com**

Printed in the United States of America.

Table of Contents

Addition with Sums Through 20

Subtraction Through 20

Addition and Subtraction Through 20

Sums with More Than Two Addends

Skip Counting for Pre-Multiplication

Rod Word Problems

Student Worksheets and Masters

Addition and Subtraction with Cuisenaire® Rods consists of:

- 83 learning experiences that provide teaching ideas, student activities and games at the concrete level, and support for the worksheets;
- 92 student worksheets for practice at the pictorial and numerical levels; and
- 16 worksheet masters for ease in providing additional problems.

Although this book is intended primarily for grades 1 and 2, it is topic-oriented and can be used at any grade level in which the concepts are being taught. Teachers and students do not require previous experience with Cuisenaire Rods. Well-developed sections on familiarity with rods and transitions from rods to numerals provide the needed rod experiences that lead naturally into work on addition and subtraction.

The title of each learning experience serves to describe the activity. The materials needed are listed at the top of each teacher page. The settings within which the experience can best be implemented are also described. Each experience has as its foundation important underlying mathematical concepts. These concepts are carefully defined and may serve as behavioral objectives.

Learning Experiences, Student Worksheets, and Masters

The 83 learning experiences are of two types: 36 of them provide activities and games for the students; the other 47 provide lessons for introducing the worksheets, give examples to help illustrate the work to be done by the students, and provide answers to the problems on the worksheets.

As each learning experience is described, the roles of the teacher and the students are stated simply and clearly. Any special accommodations to make the activity more suitable for a particular age or type of learner are shared. Whenever appropriate, discussion questions are suggested to focus the experience and to reinforce the concepts of the lesson.

The format of the worksheets is also very straightforward. Directions are given for the teacher to read to the students. Older students will be able to read the directions themselves. The coloring exercises help students learn the mathematical concepts and provide fun, plus a sense of accomplishment. In fact, many students enjoy the coloring activities so much that they often choose to color more than what is required on the worksheets. Older students, who may not be thrilled about coloring, may simply indicate the colors to be used by a splotch of color or by writing the rod codes.

Many of the learning experiences lend themselves to independent investigations. A teacher may wish to provide directions on an activity card or tape recorder so that students may work on their own in an activity area. This is especially helpful as a means of extending the ideas for the more able students. Review lessons can be provided in this manner for students who have been absent or who may need further practice. The worksheet masters can be used by both teachers and students to create problems for further practice. These sheets lend themselves to both acceleration and remediation and may be duplicated numerous times for different uses.

For the concepts of whole number addition and subtraction, white rods are used to measure the other rod lengths. The relationship of each rod length to the number of matching white rods provides a framework for the number work. Careful transitions are made from experience with rods to work with numbers by means of students coloring rod lengths on strips gridded in centimeters and by placing rods on number lines gridded in centimeters. The pictorial stage firmly establishes the number relationships in terms of white rods and is carried through the entire development of addition and subtraction concepts. Teachers should recognize, however, that many rod activities, in particular fraction concepts, will involve measuring with rods other than white, and hence there are constant reminders to students that the numbers being represented evolve in terms of white rods as the unit of measure.

Materials

The materials needed for each learning experience are clearly specified at the top of each learning experience page. A minimum of materials is needed to do the activities and worksheets. The teacher and students need only Cuisenaire Rods to proceed. Other supportive materials used from time to time throughout the text are simple and easily accessible in most classrooms.

Optional Materials for the Teacher

- **Cuisenaire Rods Template**—a plastic template that outlines in actual sizes each of the ten rod lengths. The template is excellent for making your own Cuisenaire Rod pattern designs or worksheets. (ETA 020310)
- **Cuisenaire Rods for the Overhead Projector**—a set of 60 plastic, transparent, color-coded rods. Although these are not intended to replace in any way the actual hands-on experiences with rods, they can help teachers introduce new activities and can provide another means for students to share discoveries. (ETA 4211)
- **Cuisenaire Rods Rack**—this L-shaped rack can help students line up and organize their Cuisenaire Rods. (ETA 034140)
- **Cuisenaire Rods Stamps**—a set of rubber stamps that outline in actual sizes each of the ten rod lengths. The stamps can be used for making your own Cuisenaire Rods pattern designs or worksheets. (ETA 4215)

Settings

The appropriate settings for each learning experience are listed at the top of each teacher page to help teachers implement each activity. Since students learn in a variety of situations, options for alternative settings are suggested.

Most of the activities designated as teacher-led can be completed individually or in small groups once the ideas are introduced. Students working as partners allow teachers to aid other students who may require more individualized attention. Favorite games can be repeated and varied throughout the year; minor variations to something familiar help to create a spirit of continuity and a sense of motivation. Most of the activities and games can be enjoyed during free time and need not take place during mathematics class periods.

The various settings all presume interaction with rods. Hands-on experiences with rods should be the major emphasis for the activities and games. In their mathematical experiences, students display powerful intuitions and logical strategies at the concrete stage. Students should formulate and discuss ideas prior to expressing them in written notation. The notation (codes and numerals) should serve only the function of recording that which the students already know. For many of the worksheets, the students use rods to check their problems rather than to solve the problems. The self-checking nature of the work with rods helps students to become self-reliant and self-confident.

Underlying Mathematics

A very important feature of this book is the clearly designated mathematical principles underlying each activity. These serve as an overview of both content and process and are tied to the *Principles and Standards for School Mathematics* published in 2000 by the National Council of Teachers of Mathematics to include the processes of problem solving, reasoning and proof, communication, connections, and representations along with the appropriate content.

- Association of codes with rods (pp. 22–24, 26, 30, 43–45, 47–53, 71–72, 91, 95)

- Association of codes with words (pp. 30, 91)

- Association of colors with lengths (pp. 19–20, 23, 27–30, 42, 63)

- Association of colors with rods (pp. 13–19, 22–24, 26, 41)

- Association of numbers with rods (pp. 25, 27–28, 32–33, 55, 58–61, 73–76)

- Association of rods with codes (pp. 22–24, 26, 29–30, 44–45, 47–48, 89, 91)

- Association of sums with addends (pp. 46–51, 53, 55–61, 79–84, 90, 92–94)

- Association of three-dimensional rods and two-dimensional representations (pp. 17–19, 24, 35, 34, 37, 43)

- Association of various addends for a sum (pp. 42–43, 52, 54, 79)

- Awareness of rod attributes (length, color, and shape) (pp. 13–21, 63)

- Communication and verbalization of findings (pp. 34, 36–40, 43–46)

- Communication and verbalization of ideas (pp. 13–24, 30–31, 35, 41–42, 47–48, 52–54, 60, 62–65, 67–73, 77–81, 83–95)

- Commutative property of addition (pp. 43, 53–54, 56, 60, 83)

- Comparisons of lengths (pp. 20–21, 34–41)

- Concept of zero (pp. 61, 66, 70)

- Connections between arithmetic and geometry (p. 92)

- Connections between missing addends, addition, and subtraction (pp. 62–72, 74–76, 85–89)

- Connections to real-life experiences (pp. 13–18, 30, 91, 95)

- Counting (pp. 13–14, 16, 23, 25, 27–29, 31–33, 41, 45, 77–78, 82, 84, 91)

- Equality (pp. 38–40, 70)

- Even and odd numbers (pp. 31–33, 83, 95)

- Horizontal and vertical orientations (pp. 16, 18)

- Inequalities (greater than) (pp. 36–40, 70)

- Inequalities (less than) (pp. 34–35, 38–40, 70)

- Meaning of addition (pp. 41–47, 49–51, 55–61, 83)

Exploring the Rods

Materials
Cuisenaire Rods for each student

Settings
One student working individually
A small group, students working individually
A whole class, students working individually

Learning Experience

Ask each student to take some rods and explore them. Let students work on their own for some time. They will do a wide variety of things. Some students will sort by colors. They may be interested in what is included in the set of 74 Cuisenaire Rods (22 white rods, 12 red rods, 10 green rods, 6 purple rods, and 4 each of the yellow, dark green, black, brown, blue, and orange rods). Some students will build flat designs. Some will build tall structures, which may crash and need to be rebuilt. Some will organize the rods by lengths in staircase patterns and may be aware of the ten colors going from the shortest rod (white) to the longest rod (orange).

Students should be encouraged to share ideas with each other. When it seems appropriate, informally direct students' explorations with questions, such as:

- *What did you make? How many rods did it take? Did you use all the colors?*

- *What do you notice about the rods? How are the rods alike? How are the rods different?*

- *How many colors are there? Can you name the colors?*

- *How many lengths are there? Does the same color always have the same length? Does the same length always have the same color?*

Exploring the rods is important, even if students are already familiar with rods from previous learning experiences. Students will engage spontaneously in further exploration in conjunction with more structured activities from the worksheets. It is through informal exploration with rods that students develop intuitions for later mathematical work.

Underlying Mathematics Related to the NCTM Standards:
Awareness of rod attributes (length, color, and shape)
Association of colors with rods
Recognition of equivalences of lengths
Counting
Connections to real-life experiences
Communication and verbalization of ideas

Working Together

Materials

Three sets of 74 Cuisenaire Rods for each group

Settings

A small group, students working together
A whole class, students working in small groups

Learning Experience

Ask the students in each group to put three sets of Cuisenaire Rods in the center of the table. Each group builds a project as a team. The students develop a theme of their own creation. Two challenges should be given to add more fun and creative thinking:

1) Students can only use the rods from their own table and cannot borrow any rods from another table.

2) Students must think of uses for all of the rods.

Some typical themes that students enjoy building are:
• Our neighborhood
• A family
• A spaceship
• The four seasons
• An amusement park
• A volcano
• A farm
• A circus
• A playground
• A zoo
• Various flowers, fruits, or vegetables
• A city with skyscrapers
• A birthday party

• An airport
• Various sports
• Animals and their habitats
• Musical instruments
• Characters and scenes from familiar children's stories
• People who help us (policemen, nurses, firemen, etc.)

Children enjoy telling stories about their projects. They love to tell about every aspect of their creations. This activity provides many opportunities for integration with other subject areas, such as reading, social studies, language arts, science, and art. It is nice to photograph each project and the students involved. Both the stories and photographs can be shared with parents.

Students can put the rods back into individual sets either by counting the number of rods of each color in a typical set or by sorting the rods by color and dividing them equally into three sets.

Underlying Mathematics Related to the NCTM Standards:

Awareness of rod attributes (length, color, and shape)
Association of colors with rods
Recognition of equivalences of lengths
Counting
Connections to real-life experiences
Communication and verbalization of ideas

Building Staircases

Materials
Cuisenaire Rods for each student
Ruler for each student

Settings
A small group led by the teacher
A whole class led by the teacher

Learning Experience

Ask each student to take one rod of each of the ten colors and to build a staircase. They may use a ruler to help establish a base line. The ten rods should be put in order according to their lengths.

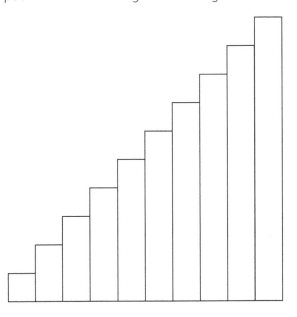

Ask the students to name the color of each rod in order from shortest to longest while looking at and touching the rods in their staircase patterns: *white, red, green, purple, yellow, dark green, black, brown, blue, orange*

Naming the colors of the rods in order can be an exciting group experience when a teacher leads the chants in unison. For fun, increase the speed each time the names of the colors are chanted.

Students may wish to continue building their staircases down from orange to white. As a challenge, name the rods from white to orange going up the staircase, and then from orange to white going down the staircase. When students feel ready, they may wish to close their eyes while naming the colors.

Some students may enjoy naming the sequence in another way; for example, thinking of flavors that correspond to the colors, such as: *vanilla, strawberry, lime, grape, lemon, spearmint, licorice, chocolate, blueberry, orange*

Encourage students to think of other ideas that will help them remember the color sequence.

Underlying Mathematics Related to the NCTM Standards:
Awareness of rod attributes (length, color, and shape)
Association of colors with rods
Ordering lengths
Recognition of rod lengths
Visual memory of shapes
Connections to real-life experiences
Communication and verbalization of ideas

Building Flat Designs

Materials

Cuisenaire Rods for each student
Unlined paper (optional)

Settings

One student working individually
A small group, students working individually
A whole class, students working individually

Learning Experience

Ask each student to build an object or design so that the rods remain flat on the table or floor. Rods may be placed horizontally, vertically, or at an angle to each other, but they may not be placed on top of each other.

Two rods at an angle to each other

Vertical

Horizontal

Students may want to make an interesting picture by putting the rods on a sheet of unlined paper. The paper provides a workspace, which some students need to define the task. Some students will build a free-form design. Others may depict something familiar, such as a truck, an airplane, a boat, a clown, a dragon, a giraffe, a robot, a monster, a dinosaur, a letter of the alphabet, or a numeral.

This activity provides an opportunity for students to learn words related to relative positions in space, such as *next to, to the left of, to the right of, beside, below, above, touching, not touching*, etc.

In their free exploration with rods, students often create designs that are symmetrical, like the tree and flower on page 97 or the robot on page 98. The portions of the design on both sides of a line of symmetry match. Students should be encouraged to make symmetrical designs and to think of examples of symmetry in real life, such as objects in nature, architecture, paintings, and interior decorations. This activity can help students become more aware of shape and form in their environment.

Underlying Mathematics Related to the NCTM Standards:

Awareness of rod attributes (length, color, and shape)
Association of colors with rods
Recognition of equivalences of lengths
Horizontal and vertical orientations

Counting
Symmetry
Connections to real-life experiences
Communication and verbalization of ideas

Making Rod Pictures

Materials

Cuisenaire Rods for each student
Crayons matching the rod colors for each student
Making Rod Pictures:
    Worksheet 1, page 97
    Worksheet 2, page 98
Cuisenaire Rods Template (optional)

Settings

One student working individually
A small group, students working individually
A whole class, students working individually

Learning Experience

The worksheets on pages 97 and 98 are the first in a series that make the transition from concrete work with rods to pictorial representations. The learning experiences on pages 13–16 are prerequisite to these worksheets.

Students should first estimate which rod fits on each rod picture and then check by placing the rod on top of each rod picture. Some students may have to try several rods before finding the correct rod. However, once some of the rod lengths are known, they serve as a frame of reference for estimating the other rods more readily.

In coloring the lengths, some students may proceed one rod at a time. Others may remove all the rods and color the whole picture by remembering the colors. If you do not have two shades of green in your set of crayons, the students can shade lightly the light green rod pictures and color hard to make the dark green pictures.

Younger students may have trouble coloring neatly within the outlines. This is of little concern, since the emphasis is on the association of color with length. The purpose of these coloring exercises is to help students go from the three-dimensional rods to a two-dimensional representation of them. With the aid of a Cuisenaire Rods Template, the students or teacher can make more sheets like these.

Solutions

These sheets are self-checking. To verify their work, students should look at the color used, get the rod of that color, and check that it matches the picture. They should leave the pictures of white rods uncolored.

Making Rod Pictures Worksheet 1 (p. 97)
Hi: dark green, red, dark green, white, green
Boat: brown, orange, orange, blue, brown
Tree: white, red, green, purple, yellow, red, red
Puppy: red, purple, purple, white, white
Flower: red, red, red, dark green, green, green

Making Rod Pictures Worksheet 2 (p. 98)
House: purple, purple, green, purple, purple, purple
Robot: red, green, white, purple, white, green, green, green, white, white
Staircase pattern: blue, black, yellow, green, white, red, purple, dark green, brown, orange
Dog: red, red, blue, dark green, dark green, red, green

Underlying Mathematics Related to the NCTM Standards:
Awareness of rod attributes (length, color, and shape)
Association of colors with rods
Association of three-dimensional rods and two-dimensional representations
Visual memory of shapes
Symmetry
Reasoning and proof
Connections to real-life experiences
Communication and verbalization of ideas

Building and Coloring on Graph Paper

Materials

Cuisenaire Rods for each student
Crayons matching the rod colors for each student
1-cm Graph Paper Master, page 99

Settings

One student working individually
A small group, students working individually
A whole class, students working individually

Learning Experience

Photocopy a sheet of centimeter graph paper for each student, using the master on page 99. Ask each student to build a flat design on the graph paper. Students may need to be shown the proper placement of rods. In this activity, each rod must be placed so that it is horizontal or vertical and covers entire squares.

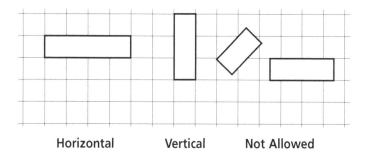

| Horizontal | Vertical | Not Allowed |

Ask students to color an exact picture of their designs. Demonstrate how to remove one rod at a time and how to color the squares that it covered with the appropriate color. To show a white rod, students should darken the outline of a centimeter square and leave the square uncolored. Once all rods have been removed and their spaces colored, ask students to check their pictures by using the colors to rebuild the design.

Students will make a wide variety of designs. Their designs should be shared and discussed. Generally, it is easier for young students to match rods to colored pictures than it is to color a rod picture. If this is a difficult activity, students can build designs on top of graph paper pictures made by others. Coloring rod lengths on centimeter graph paper helps students build readiness for number work where the white rod represents 1. All the designs made in this activity should be kept for later addition experiences, such as the learning experience on page 92.

Underlying Mathematics Related to the NCTM Standards:

Awareness of rod attributes (length, color, and shape)
Recognition of rod lengths
Association of colors with rods
Horizontal and vertical orientations
Association of three-dimensional rods and two-dimensional representations
Connections to real-life experiences
Communication and verbalization of ideas

Materials

Cuisenaire Rods for each student
Crayons matching the rod colors for each student
1-cm Graph Paper Master, page 99

Settings

A small group led by the teacher
A whole class led by the teacher

Learning Experience

Photocopy a sheet of centimeter graph paper for each student, using the master on page 99. Ask each student to use one rod of each color to build a staircase from shortest (white) to longest (orange) on the centimeter graph paper. Direct students to mark the ends of each rod and to color its length with the correct color. Once the staircases are colored, ask the students to chant the colors of the rods in unison, with rhythm: *white, red, green, pur-ple, yel-low, dark-green, black, brown, blue, or-ange*

A series of developmental steps might include:

1) Chanting the colors of the five shortest rods
   • while looking at and touching the colored staircase picture
   • while only looking at the colored staircase picture
   • with eyes closed
   • in reverse order (yellow, purple, green, red, white)

2) Chanting the colors of the five longest rods
   • forwards (dark green, black, brown, blue, orange)
   • in reverse order (orange, blue, brown, black, dark green)

3) Chanting all ten colors
   • forwards (white, red, green, purple, yellow, dark green, black, brown, blue, orange)
   • in reverse order (orange, blue, brown, black, dark green, yellow, purple, green, red, white)

Repeating each chant several times in succession helps students know the sequence of the rod colors more automatically. Activities directed toward learning the sequence of rod colors should be done for short periods of time over several sessions.

<u>Underlying Mathematics Related to the NCTM Standards:</u>

Awareness of rod attributes (length, color, and shape)
Association of colors with rods
Association of colors with lengths
Ordering lengths
Visual memory of shapes
Association of three-dimensional rods and two-dimensional representations
Communication and verbalization of ideas

Guessing the Rods

Materials
Cuisenaire Rods for each student
Empty container for each pair of students

Settings
Two students working together
A small group, students working in pairs
A whole class, students working in pairs

Learning Experience

Ask each student to make a staircase using one rod of each color. Have partners place the ten rods from one of the staircases in an empty container and shake it to mix them. The other staircase should be left in plain sight on the table.

Direct the first student to name one of the ten rods. Ask the second student to reach inside the container to find that rod by touching and not looking. (The second student may look at the staircase on the table for help.) The rod is taken out and both students check to see that the named rod has been chosen. If not, the second student tries again. The same rods are put back into the container. Have students take turns naming and finding rods.

When they feel confident, a more challenging game can be played. Have the first student put his hand behind his back, and the second student place one of the rods from the container in the first student's hand. The first student tries to guess the rod by touching it and not looking at it. The first student may, however, touch the rod with both hands (in order to feel the full length of the rod) and look at the staircase on the table. Two guesses are allowed. The rod is then put back into the container. Have students take turns and keep score of correct guesses. They may want to take note of the rods that they miss on their first guess. Usually, the five shortest rods are easier than the five longest rods.

Underlying Mathematics Related to the NCTM Standards:
Awareness of rod attributes (length, color, and shape)
Recognition of rod lengths
Ordering lengths
Association of colors with lengths
Comparisons of lengths
Visual memory of shapes
Communication and verbalization of ideas

Playing the Staircase Game

Materials
Cuisenaire Rods for each pair of students
Ruler for each student
Empty container for each pair of students

Settings
Two students working together
A small group, students working in pairs
A whole class, students working in pairs

Learning Experience

Have partners place two rods of each color into an empty container. As students place the rods into the container, have them name the colors:

two white, two red, two green, two purple, two yellow, two dark green, two black, two brown, two blue, two orange

Ask one student to shake the container so that the rods are thoroughly mixed. Taking turns, have each student reach into the container and take out a rod without looking. The rods must be taken out in order from shortest to longest. As a correct rod is drawn, it is placed against a ruler that serves as a baseline for forming the staircase. If the rod is not the next rod in the staircase, the student must put the rod back into

the container and wait for his or her next turn to select the correct rod length. The first student to build a staircase in order from shortest to longest wins. Students will enjoy playing this game several times.

As a variation, have both students build their staircases in order from longest to shortest. As they gain proficiency, students may enjoy the challenge of having one student build from shortest to longest while the other builds from longest to shortest. Students should swap roles from game to game.

Underlying Mathematics Related to the NCTM Standards:
Awareness of rod attributes (length, color, and shape)
Recognition of rod lengths
Ordering lengths
Comparisons of lengths
Visual memory of shapes
Communication and verbalization of ideas

Learning the Codes

Materials

Cuisenaire Rods for each student
10 index cards for the teacher

Settings

A small group led by the teacher
A whole class led by the teacher

Learning Experience

As work with rods progresses, it is natural to write down some of the discoveries. In recording these for the students, the teacher often uses shortcuts like 2 for "two," + for "plus," = for "equals," etc. Many students in class may have nicknames that are shorter than their first names. Also, initials are often used as abbreviations for our full names. It will become just as natural to use abbreviations for the rod colors.

When a student tells you "two white rods equal a red rod," you may initially write:

2 white rods = 1 red rod

But soon, the discoveries will come from students so quickly that it is helpful to be able to record their responses rapidly. The usual convention is to use a single letter to stand for the color name, such as 2W = 1R. When alphabet symbols are used, the preceding example is read as "2 white rods = 1 red rod."

For the first six rods, the first letters of the color names are written:
W for White   R for Red   G for Green
P for Purple   Y for Yellow   D for Dark green

The black, brown, and blue rods all begin with the same first letter; hence their last letters are used for the code.
K for blacK   N for browN   E for bluE

Notice that the 𝒪 for Orange should have a tail on it to distinguish it from the symbol for zero. A chart may be made for the bulletin board such as the one shown below:

W	for	White	D	for	Dark green
R	for	Red	K	for	blacK
G	for	Green	N	for	browN
P	for	Purple	E	for	bluE
Y	for	Yellow	𝒪	for	Orange

Using ten index cards, make a deck of cards with the code letters on them. Hold up a card. Ask students to hold up the appropriate rod and say the correct color name. Let students self-correct if they don't get the correct rod on the first try. Seeing other students' answers will help reinforce the association of rods with codes. Do this activity several times, speeding up the pace with which the students must find the correct rod to match the code.

Underlying Mathematics Related to the NCTM Standards:
Association of colors with rods
Association of codes with rods
Association of rods with codes
Visual memory of shapes
Communication and verbalization of ideas

Playing Games with Codes

Materials

Cuisenaire Rods for each group
30 index cards for each group
Empty container for each group

Settings

A small group working together
A whole class working in small groups

Learning Experience

Make a deck of 30 cards consisting of 3 cards of each of the 10 rod codes: W, R, G, P, Y, D, K, N, E, and O. One player in each group acts as a dealer and does not play. The dealer shuffles the deck of code cards and deals five cards face down to each person. Each player hides his or her cards so that the others cannot see them. The dealer stacks the remaining cards face down in the center of the table. The dealer places one rod of each color into a container.

The dealer says "Go" and takes a rod from the container. The first player to put the correct code card face up in the center of the table wins the card as score. The rod is put back into the container. This player draws another card from the playing deck in the center of the table. If no one has the correct card, the dealer puts the rod back into the container and selects a different rod. The game ends when all the cards from the playing deck have been used. The player who has collected the most cards wins. The remaining cards in the players' hands are not counted as part of the score.

As a variation, the dealer shuffles the deck of cards and places it face down in the center of the table. Then he gives each player one rod of each of the ten colors. On each round, the dealer turns one card face up. The first player to put the correct rod on top of this code card wins the card and recovers the rod to use in future turns. The game ends when the deck of cards runs out. The player who has accumulated the most cards wins.

These games are enjoyable for students to play during free time and need not be played during scheduled mathematics time.

Underlying Mathematics Related to the NCTM Standards:

Association of colors with lengths
Association of colors with rods
Association of codes with rods
Association of rods with codes
Counting
Communication and verbalization of ideas

Practicing Rod Codes

Materials
Cuisenaire Rods for each student
Crayons matching the rod colors for each student
Pencil for each student
Practicing Rod Codes:
    Worksheet 1, page 100
    Worksheet 2, page 101
Cuisenaire Rods Template (optional)

Settings
One student working individually
A small group, students working individually
A whole class, students working individually

Learning Experience
The worksheets on pages 100 and 101 link the rod codes to pictorial representations of the rods. The learning experiences on pages 20–23 are prerequisite to these worksheets. A bulletin board or poster similar to the rod code chart pictured on page 100 can be made.

Students should first estimate which rod fits on each picture and then check their estimate by putting the rod on top. While saying the color name, they should write the code for the color name. The codes can be written on or beside each rod picture with a pencil or with the crayon of the correct color. Some students may need guidance as they begin this activity.

Students enjoy going back to the worksheets on pages 97 and 98 and writing codes next to these pictures. More rod pictures can be made with the aid of the Cuisenaire Rods Template.

Solutions

These worksheets are self-checking. To verify their work, students should look at the picture, get the rod of that color, check that it matches the picture, and check the codes from the chart.

Practicing Rod Codes Worksheet 1 (p. 100)
Stop sign: red, red, red, red, red, red, red, red; R, R, R, R, R, R, R, R
Hat: purple, purple, purple, purple, dark green; P, P, P, P, D
Letter L: blue, yellow; E, Y
Staircase: orange, blue, brown, black, dark green, yellow, purple, green, red, white; O, E, N, K, D, Y, P, G, R, W

Practicing Rod Codes Worksheet 2 (page 101)
Symmetrical design: P, R, G, G, R, P, O, O, P, R, G, G, R, P
Key: K, R, R, K
Truck: G, G, R, Y, P, R, E, W, W
Letter A: E, G, E

Underlying Mathematics Related to the NCTM Standards:
Association of colors with rods
Association of codes with rods
Association of rods with codes
Association of three-dimensional rods and two-dimensional representations
Reasoning and proof
Communication and verbalization of ideas

Matching Each Rod with White Rods

Materials
Cuisenaire Rods for each student

Settings
A small group led by the teacher
A whole class led by the teacher

Learning Experience

Ask each student to take one rod at a time and count how many white rods are needed to match each rod. For example:

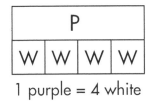

1 purple = 4 white

This activity provides counting experience for young students. It also gives them the opportunity to establish equivalences. For example:

1 red = 2 white; 1 green = 3 white;
1 yellow = 5 white; 1 dark green = 6 white;
1 black = 7 white; 1 brown = 8 white;
1 blue = 9 white; and 1 orange = 10 white

Once all the matches have been made, ask students to chant the number of white rods associated with each rod. Then name a color and have them respond with the number of matching white rods (e.g., you say "blue rod," and they answer "9 white rods"). Then say a number of white rods and have them respond with the correct rod color (e.g., you say "6 white rods," and they answer "dark green rod"). Students should be encouraged to prove their answers by counting the number of white rods matching the rod lengths.

It is important to note the distinction between saying that 1 yellow = 5 white (a statement that is always true) and saying that yellow = 5 (a statement that would be true only if the white rod is considered to be 1).

If orange is considered as 1, then yellow would be $\frac{1}{2}$. The beauty of the rods comes from the fact that numbers can be assigned to the rod relationships to teach both early and more advanced mathematics.

Since most of the work in this book focuses on whole numbers, the relationship between each rod to white rods is the most important use of the rod model. Hence, the following activities focus on the length of each rod in terms of white rods.

Underlying Mathematics Related to the NCTM Standards:
Recognition of equivalences of lengths
Representation of lengths in terms of white rods
Counting
Association of numbers with rods
Reasoning and proof

Matching Codes and Rods

Materials
Cuisenaire Rods for each student
Crayons matching the rod colors for each student
Matching Codes and Rods:
Worksheet 1, page 102
Worksheet 2, page 103

Settings
One student working individually
A small group, students working individually
A whole class, students working individually

Learning Experience
The worksheets on pages 102 and 103 review the rod codes. Students should look at the rod code, say the color name, get the rod, place it on the strip, and color its length the correct color. They should be reminded that the left end of the rod should be placed at the beginning of the strip. Since the strips are gridded by the length of a white rod, students can color the length of each rod by counting the number of white rods equivalent to the rod, rather than estimating visually.

These worksheets show pictorially the relationship of each rod to the number of white rods that match it, and provide a means of recording the learning experience on page 25. This work is prerequisite for the more abstract stage of using numerals.

Solutions

These worksheets are self-checking—students can verify their work by looking at the color and finding the corresponding rod to place on the strip. Having students check their work on a second day means that each worksheet can provide two worthwhile experiences. The number of squares to be colored is the number of white rods that matches the length of each rod.

Matching Codes and Rods Worksheet 1 (p. 102)
1) purple	P = 4W
2) black	K = 7W
3) red	R = 2W
4) yellow	Y = 5W
5) green	G = 3W
6) orange	O = 10W
7) brown	N = 8W
8) blue	E = 9W

Matching Codes and Rods Worksheet 2 (p. 103)
1) purple	P = 4W
2) white	W = 1W
3) dark green	D = 6W
4) red	R = 2W
5) orange	O = 10W
6) brown	N = 8W
7) blue	E = 9W
8) green	G = 3W
9) yellow	Y = 5W

Underlying Mathematics Related to the NCTM Standards:
Association of colors with rods
Association of codes with rods
Association of rods with codes
Representation of lengths in terms of white rods
Reasoning and proof

Matching Rods and Numerals

Materials

Cuisenaire Rods for each student
Crayons matching the rod colors for each student
Pencil for each student
Matching Rods and Numerals:
>Worksheet 1, page 104
>Worksheet 2, page 105

Settings

One student working individually
A small group, students working individually
A whole class, students working individually

Learning Experience

The worksheets on pages 104 and 105 extend the concrete stage of the learning experience on page 25 and the pictorial stage of the learning experience on page 26 to the more abstract stage with numerals. Notice that these worksheets do not require students to have the facility to write numerals, only to recognize them.

Encourage students to look at each rod picture and to estimate how many white rods would match it. Then have them check by covering each picture with white rods. An association of numbers in terms of white rods is reinforced as students color each picture the correct rod color.

The format of the worksheets may be difficult for those students who have perceptual and motor problems in drawing circles and lines. However, once students understand the concept, they may respond orally or point to the correct numeral.

Solutions

The worksheets are self-checking—students can verify their work by looking at the designated numeral, getting that number of white rods, matching the rod picture with them, and then replacing the white rods with a colored rod. Having the students check their own work on a second day means that each worksheet can provide two worthwhile experiences.

Matching Rods and Numerals Worksheet 1 (p. 104)
1) black   7
2) blue   9
3) red   2
4) yellow   5
5) orange   10
6) green   3
7) dark green   6
8) brown   8

Matching Rods and Numerals Worksheet 2 (p. 105)
1) red   2
2) brown   8
3) white   1
4) yellow   5
5) blue   9
6) purple   4
7) dark green   6
8) orange   10
9) green   3

Underlying Mathematics Related to the NCTM Standards:
Association of colors with lengths
Representation of lengths in terms of white rods
Counting
Association of numbers with rods
Reasoning and proof

Coloring Rod Lengths

Materials
Cuisenaire Rods for each student
Crayons matching the rod colors for each student
Coloring Rod Lengths:
Worksheet 1, page 106
Worksheet 2, page 107

Settings
One student working individually
A small group, students working individually
A whole class, students working individually

Learning Experience

The worksheets on pages 106 and 107 proceed from sets of white rods to single rods. This activity encourages the transfer from the concept of number as a discrete set of objects to the concept of number as a continuous length. In the example on page 106, 6 white rods can be thought of as 6 ones, while the dark green rod can be thought of as 1 six. Both approaches to number are important. The discrete model appeals to more analytical processing; the continuous model encourages a more perceptual approach.

In completing these worksheets, some students will put the given number of white rods end to end in a train and then find the rod that matches the train. Others will count the number of white rods represented on the strip and match a rod to that length on the strip.

The coloring stage reinforces the relationship of each rod color to the equivalent number of white rods.

Solutions

These sheets are self-checking—students can look at the colored strip, find the corresponding rod to match, and count the number of white rods.

Coloring Rod Lengths Worksheet 1 (p. 106)
1) 3W   green
2) 8W   brown
3) 5W   yellow
4) 2W   red
5) 4W   purple
6) 9W   blue
7) 7W   black
8) 10W   orange

Coloring Rod Lengths Worksheet 2 (p. 107)
1) 7W   black
2) 1W   white
3) 3W   green
4) 5W   yellow
5) 10W   orange
6) 2W   red
7) 8W   brown
8) 6W   dark green

Underlying Mathematics Related to the NCTM Standards:
Representation of lengths in terms of white rods
Association of colors with lengths
Counting
Association of numbers with rods
Reasoning and proof

Matching Codes and Lengths

Materials

Cuisenaire Rods for each student
Crayons matching the rod colors for each student
Matching Codes and Lengths Worksheet, page 108

Settings

One student working individually
A small group, students working individually
A whole class, students working individually

Learning Experience

The worksheet on page 108 is similar to the worksheets on pages 102 and 103, but this worksheet requires the students to record the number of white rods that match the rod length they have colored. Students should look at the letter code, say the color name, think of the number of white rods equivalent to that rod length, and then color the correct length. The rods are used to check answers, not to solve the problems. Many students will be able to do this with proficiency.

However, some students may still need to get the rods and match them with white rods in order to complete this worksheet. If the codes give trouble, especially K, E, and N, review how they were chosen, using page 22, then repeat the Games with Codes, using page 23. More practice with this concept will be given on future worksheets. Mastery is not expected at this stage of development.

Solutions

This worksheet is self-checking—students can verify their work by looking at the color and finding the corresponding rod to place on the strip. The number of squares to be colored is the number of white rods that match each rod.

Matching Codes and Lengths Worksheet (p. 108)
1) orange   10W
2) black   7W
3) white   1W
4) blue   9W
5) red   2W
6) brown   8W
7) yellow   5W
8) purple   4W
9) dark green   6W

Underlying Mathematics Related to the NCTM Standards:

Association of rods with codes
Association of colors with lengths
Representation of lengths in terms of white rods
Counting
Reasoning and proof

Matching Numerals and Codes

Materials

Cuisenaire Rods for each student
Pencil for each student
Matching Numerals and Codes:
  Worksheet 1, page 109
  Worksheet 2, page 110
  Master, page 111

Settings

One student working individually
A small group, students working individually
A whole class, students working individually

Learning Experience

Students will enjoy doing the worksheets on pages 109 and 110, since the codes are used to spell words. Some students will be quicker at this activity than others. For those students who don't know what rod matches a given number of white rods, encourage them to make a train of white rods and find the rod that matches the train.

Even with the limited number of letters, W, R, G, P, Y, D, K, N, E, and O, many words can be written. The more verbal students who can already spell may wish to think up some words and make similar worksheets to share with the class. They may want to think of people's names that can be made with rod codes, such as DON, NED, PEG, PEGGY, KEN, and RON.

Some sample words that can be used on the master on page 111 are: ONE, KEY, DRY, KNOW, NEW, PEN, WON, WORN, YOKE, GROWN, POKE, NONE, WEDGE, and DROWN. Given these answers, students can make up problems stating the number of white rods.

Solutions

These worksheets are self-checking—each set of problems spells a word. The worksheets also can be checked by taking each code letter, finding the corresponding rod, matching it with a train of white rods, and counting the number of white rods used.

Matching Numerals and Codes Worksheet 1 (p. 109)
1) GOOD
2) DOG
3) GO
4) DOWN
5) ROPE
6) YOYO
7) POWER

Matching Numerals and Codes Worksheet 2 (p. 110)
1) ROD
2) END
3) KEEP
4) GROW
5) POND
6) GREEN
7) PEEK
8) OWNER

Underlying Mathematics Related to the NCTM Standards:

Representation of lengths in terms of white rods
Association of colors with lengths
Association of rods with codes
Association of codes with rods

Association of codes with words
Reasoning and proof
Connections to real-life experiences
Communication and verbalization of ideas

Covering with Red Rods

Materials

Cuisenaire Rods for each student
Ruler for each student

Settings

One student working individually
A small group, students working individually
A whole class, students working individually

Learning Experience

Ask each student to take one rod at a time and to match it with red rods. Students may use a ruler to help line up the rods. They should note that some rods cannot be matched exactly by red rods.

Purple can be matched with 2 red rods.

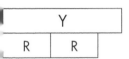 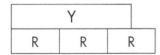

Yellow cannot be matched exactly with red rods. Two red rods are not enough and three red rods are too much.

Ask students to select those rods that can be measured by red rods and to make a staircase: red, purple, dark green, brown, and orange. This staircase starts with a red rod, and each step increases by one red rod. This staircase is often called an "even" staircase. Any rod that can be measured exactly by red rods is an even rod.

Ask the students to take the rods in an even staircase (red, purple, dark green, brown, orange) and to explore the property of evenness in another way. Have them show that each even rod can be matched exactly with two rods of the same color:

 Red can be matched with 2 white rods.

 Purple can be matched with 2 red rods.

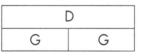 Dark green can be matched with 2 green rods.

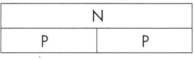 Brown can be matched with 2 purple rods.

Orange can be matched with 2 yellow rods.

This activity builds readiness for the concept that every even number is twice another whole number. The rods that are not even (white, green, yellow, black, blue) are called odd. Have students show that none of the odd rods can be matched exactly with a train of red rods or two rods of the same color. Students may enjoy looking again at the odd and even staircase pattern in Exercise 3 on page 98.

Underlying Mathematics Related to the NCTM Standards:

Representation of equivalences of lengths
Representation of lengths in terms of red rods
Counting
Even and odd numbers
Reasoning and proof
Communication and verbalization of ideas

Building with Red Rods

Materials
Cuisenaire Rods for each student

Settings
A small group led by the teacher
A whole class led by the teacher

Learning Experience
Ask each student to build a staircase using only red rods. Each step in the staircase increases by one red rod.

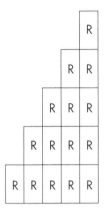

Ask each student to find one rod that matches each step in the staircase.

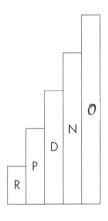

You might ask students the following questions:

• *Does each of the ten rod colors match a step?* [no]

• *Which of the ten rod colors do you use?* [red, purple, dark green, brown, orange]

• *If the red rod were used as the "measuring" rod, what value would each step in the staircase have?* [1, 2, 3, 4, 5] In this example, the red rod has a value of 1.

• *If the white rod were the "measuring" rod, what value would each step in the staircase have?* [2, 4, 6, 8, 10] In this example, the white rod has a value of 1.

This activity shows that the first five even numbers are 2, 4, 6, 8, and 10. Each even number is two more than the previous one, since each step in the staircase increases by a red rod. The next length after 10 would be equivalent to 12 white rods; the next, 14; the next, 16; the next, 18; etc. Having students add successive red rods while counting up by two helps them build readiness for the concept of multiplication as repeated addition.

NCTM
BASED ON
STANDARDS

Underlying Mathematics Related to the NCTM Standards:
Recognition of equivalences of lengths
Representation of lengths in terms of red rods
Counting
Association of numbers with rods
Skip counting by twos
Multiplication as repeated addition
Even and odd numbers

Matching Rods with Red Rods

Materials

Cuisenaire Rods for each student
Crayons matching the rod colors for each student
Matching Rods with Red Rods Worksheet, page 112

Settings

One student working individually
A small group, students working individually
A whole class, students working individually

Learning Experience

The worksheet on page 112 gives students the opportunity to use red rods to measure other rods. Along with the previous learning experiences on pages 31 and 32, it encourages students to discover that the number values associated with the rods are not fixed.

Even young students should have a few experiences in which the white rod is not always 1 and the orange rod is not always 10. Without this preparation, later topics, such as fractions and decimals, will be more difficult.

When this worksheet is completed, students should notice that if the red rod were 1, then purple would be 2; dark green, 3; brown, 4; and orange, 5. Another interesting observation is that the number of centimeter squares colored in terms of red rods is always an even number: 2, 4, 6, 8, 10, etc.

Solutions

This worksheet is self-checking—students can look at the colored strip, find the corresponding rod to match, and count the number of red rods that match.

Matching Rods with Red Rods Worksheet (p. 112)
1) red   covers 2 squares
2) brown   covers 8 squares
3) purple   covers 4 squares
4) orange   covers 10 squares
5) dark green   covers 6 squares
     rod words   ROD, POOR

Underlying Mathematics Related to the NCTM Standards:

Recognition of equivalences of lengths
Representation of lengths in terms of red rods
Counting
Association of numbers with rods
Even and odd numbers
Skip counting by twos
Multiplication as repeated addition
Reasoning and proof

Finding Rods "Less Than"

Materials
Cuisenaire Rods for each student
Cuisenaire Rods for the teacher

Settings
A small group led by the teacher
A whole class led by the teacher

Learning Experience

Choose a green rod and a brown rod and place them side by side.

Like this...

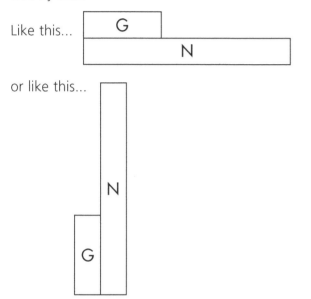

or like this...

Students should discover that the green rod is less than the brown rod since the green rod is shorter than the brown rod.

Ask students to find other rods less than the brown rod. Students should be able to prove the inequality by placing the rods side by side.

In finding all rods less than a given rod, some students will discover that it is possible to select an appropriate portion of a staircase. For example, if students are asked to find all the rods less than the brown rod, they could give the answer as white through black in the staircase; in other words, white, red, green, purple, yellow, dark green, and black.

An interesting activity involves having students take a handful of rods and asking: *All of these rods are less than what rod?* All the possible correct answers should be given.

Two other interesting questions are the following:

• *Is there any rod that has no rods less than it?* [white]

• *Is there any rod less than all other rods?* [white]

Underlying Mathematics Related to the NCTM Standards:
Inequalities (less than)
Comparisons of lengths
Ordering lengths
Reasoning and proof
Communication and verbalization of findings

Practicing "Less Than"

Materials

Cuisenaire Rods for each student
Crayons matching the rod colors for each student
Pencil for each student
Practicing "Less Than":
    Worksheet 1, page 113
    Worksheet 2, page 114
    Worksheet 3, page 115
    Master, page 116

Settings

One student working individually
A small group, students working individually
A whole class, students working individually

Learning Experience

Comparing rods helps students establish the order of rods and later the order of numbers. The series of worksheets on pages 113–115 carefully develops the concept of less than. As the worksheets proceed, the perceptual clues become less direct.

Some students may need to be reminded that one end of each of the rods being compared must line up. Others will not need rods at all and will be able to work exclusively in the pictorial stage. On occasion, students should be asked to prove their answers by using rods.

The exercises on the worksheets may have more than one correct answer. It is important for students to experience mathematical situations in which there is more than one correct answer. Either the teacher or the students can pose additional problems as needed using the master on page 116.

Solutions

All possible answers are given. To show a white rod, the student should outline one centimeter square and leave it uncolored.

Practicing "Less Than" Worksheet 1 (p. 113)
1) white (The rod pictured is a red rod.)
2) white, red, green, purple, yellow, dark green, black, brown (The rod pictured is a blue rod.)
3) white, red, green, purple (The rod pictured is a yellow rod.)
4) white, red, green (The rod pictured is a purple rod.)
5) white, red, green, purple, yellow, dark green, black, brown, blue (The rod pictured is an orange rod.)

Practicing "Less Than" Worksheet 2 (p. 114)
The rod pictured is a blue rod. The rods that should be circled and colored are dark green, red, yellow, purple, brown, green, white, and black.

Practicing "Less Than" Worksheet 3 (p. 115)
The rod pictured is the dark green rod. The rods that should be circled and colored are white, red, purple, yellow, and green.

Underlying Mathematics Related to the NCTM Standards:
Association of three-dimensional rods and two-dimensional representations
Inequalities (less than)
Comparisons of lengths
Ordering lengths
Reasoning and proof
Communication and verbalization of ideas

Finding Rods "Greater Than"

Materials

Cuisenaire Rods for each student
Cuisenaire Rods for the teacher

Settings

A small group led by the teacher
A whole class led by the teacher

Learning Experience

Choose a blue rod and a yellow rod and place them side by side.

Like this...

or like this...

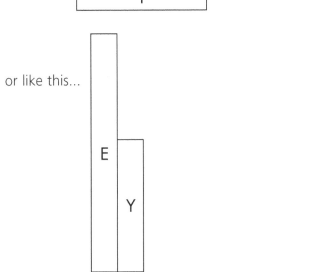

The students will find that the blue rod is greater than the yellow rod.

Hold up another rod and have the students respond by holding up any rod greater than it. Have students prove each inequality by placing the rods side by side.

In finding all rods greater than a given rod, some students will discover that it is possible to select an appropriate portion of a staircase. For example, if students are asked to find all the rods greater than the yellow rod, they could give the answer as dark green through orange in the staircase—in other words, dark green, black, brown, blue, and orange.

An interesting activity involves having the students take a handful of rods and asking: *All of these rods are greater than what rod?* All the possible correct answers should be given.

Two other interesting questions are the following:

- *Is there any rod that has no single rod greater than it?* [orange]

- *Is there any rod greater than all other rods?* [orange]

Students should be encouraged to ask each other questions so that they have the opportunity to use the vocabulary of greater than and less than.

Underlying Mathematics Related to the NCTM Standards:

Inequalities (greater than)
Comparisons of lengths
Ordering lengths
Reasoning and proof
Communication and verbalization of findings

Practicing "Greater Than"

Materials

Cuisenaire Rods for each student
Crayons matching the rod colors for each student
Practicing "Greater Than":
    Worksheet 1, page 117
    Worksheet 2, page 118
    Worksheet 3, page 119
    Master, page 120

Settings

One student working individually
A small group, students working individually
A whole class, students working individually

Learning Experience

The series of worksheets on pages 117–119 extends the comparisons of rods to include the concept of greater than. As in the previous worksheets on the concept of less than, the development gradually encourages students to do the comparisons visually.

Some students may need to be reminded that one end of each of the rods being compared must line up. Other students will not need rods at all and will be able to work exclusively in the pictorial stage. On occasion, students should be asked to prove their answers by using rods.

The exercises on the worksheets may have more than one correct answer. Experiencing mathematical situations in which there is more than one right answer is important for students. This occurs again when they have to make various trains on page 41 and find various addends for a sum on page 43. The master on page 120 may be used for making additional greater-than problems as needed.

Solutions

Practicing "Greater Than" Worksheet 1 (p. 117)
All possible answers are given.
1) black, brown, blue, orange (The rod pictured is the dark green rod.)
2) orange (The rod pictured is the blue rod.)
3) red, green, purple, yellow, dark green, black, brown, blue, orange
    (The rod pictured is the white rod.)
4) dark green, black, brown, blue, orange (The rod pictured is the yellow rod.)
5) brown, blue, orange (The rod pictured is the black rod.)

Practicing "Greater Than" Worksheet 2 (p. 118)
The rod pictured is the yellow rod. The rods that should be circled and colored are orange, blue, brown, black, and dark green.

Practicing "Greater Than" Worksheet 3 (p. 119)
The rod pictured is the purple rod. The rods that should be circled and colored are orange, brown, dark green, yellow, black, and blue.

Underlying Mathematics Related to the NCTM Standards:

Association of three-dimensional rods and two-dimensional representations
Inequalities (greater than)
Comparisons of lengths
Ordering lengths
Reasoning and proof
Communication and verbalization of findings

Playing the Comparing Game

Materials
Cuisenaire Rods for each pair of students
Empty container for each student

Settings
Two students working together
A small group, students working in pairs
A whole class, students working in pairs

Learning Experience

Ask partners to share the rods so that each student has the same number of rods of each color. Place the rods into the empty containers and hold them under the table, out of sight.

One student counts to three. On the count of three, each student takes one rod from the container and places it on the table. The two rods are compared. The player with the longer rod wins both rods. If the two rods are equal in length, the rods are discarded and no one wins on that turn. The two rods are put aside. The game ends when all the rods in the containers have been used. Each partner makes a train by putting the won rods end to end. The player with the longer train wins the game.

For variation, the player with the shorter rod wins both rods, and the player with the shorter train wins the game. Students often like to alternate games. It is important that students do not get the impression that more of something is always better.

After students become proficient at this game, players may be asked to compare the two rods on a turn and tell how much longer one rod is than the other. This extension will provide readiness for the concepts of missing addends and subtraction developed on pages 62–70.

Underlying Mathematics Related to the NCTM Standards:
One-to-one correspondence
Comparisons of lengths
Inequalities (less than, greater than)
Equality
Reasoning and proof
Communication and verbalization of findings

Materials

Cuisenaire Rods for each student

Settings

A small group led by the teacher
A whole class led by the teacher

Learning Experience

Choose two rods. Ask students to place the two rods side by side and describe the relationship between the rods.

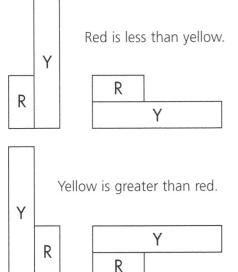

Red is less than yellow.

Yellow is greater than red.

Explain that rods are often compared, and therefore, a shorthand way of describing the relationship has been developed.

The symbol < means <u>is less than</u>.
The symbol > means <u>is greater than</u>.

These symbols can be thought of as an extension of mathematical codes.

Students should have the concepts of less than and greater than well established before learning to write the symbols. Eventually, they will develop proficiency in reading R < Y as "red is less than yellow" and Y > R as "yellow is greater than red."

Underlying Mathematics Related to the NCTM Standards:

Comparisons of lengths
Inequalities (less than, greater than)
Use of inequality signs
Equality
Reasoning and proof
Communication and verbalization of findings

Practicing Inequality Signs

Materials

Cuisenaire Rods for each student
Crayons matching the rod colors for each student
Pencil for each student
Practicing Inequality Signs:
    Worksheet 1, page 121
    Worksheet 2, page 122
    Worksheet 3, page 123

Settings

One student working individually
A small group, students working individually
A whole class, students working individually

Learning Experience

Students may need to manipulate rods in order to do these exercises, whether given pictorially, as on the worksheets on pages 121 and 122, or with numbers, as on the worksheet on page 123. The same numbers are given in reverse order on the worksheet on page 123 so that students will experience the fact that "is less than" and "is greater than" are inverse inequality relationships.

Some students will be able to work with the pictures and will not need the rods. However, they should be asked to prove selected examples with their rods.

Some students will not be able to work with the numerals alone. This is acceptable as long as the student can interpret the problem with rods and then manipulate the rods. If this occurs, it suggests that the student's ability to make the transition from pictorial to abstract processing has not yet been fully developed. This implies that the use of abstract symbols will need to be linked more closely to the concrete model.

Example: 3 < 7
Students can either compare a green rod and a black rod to see that the green rod is shorter than the black rod, or they can take three white rods and seven white rods and compare the two sets using one-to-one correspondence.

Solutions

Practicing Inequality Signs Worksheet 1 (p. 121)
1) dark green > green
2) black > yellow
3) white < green
4) black > dark green
5) dark green < brown
6) brown > black

Practicing Inequality Signs Worksheet 3 (p. 123)

1) <	**5)** <	**9)** >
2) >	**6)** >	**10)** <
3) >	**7)** >	
4) <	**8)** <	

Practicing Inequality Signs Worksheet 2 (p. 122)
There is more than one correct answer to each of these inequalities. All possible answers are given.
1) green, purple, yellow, dark green, black, brown, blue, orange
2) white, red, green, purple, yellow, dark green, black
3) red, green, purple, yellow, dark green, black, brown, blue, orange
4) white, red, green, purple, yellow, dark green
5) white, red, green
6) white, red, green, purple, yellow

Underlying Mathematics Related to the NCTM Standards:
Comparisons of lengths
Inequalities (less than, greater than)
Use of inequality signs
Equality
One-to-one correspondence
Reasoning and proof
Communication and verbalization of findings

Materials

Cuisenaire Rods for each student
Cuisenaire Rods for the teacher
Making Trains Master, page 124

Settings

A small group led by the teacher
A whole class led by the teacher

Learning Experience

Students have already been making trains by placing rods end to end. In this activity, they will make trains to meet certain conditions, such as:
• A train with four cars all the same color
• A five-car train with a dark green engine and a green caboose
• A one-car train
• A short train that has a lot of cars
• A long train that has only a few cars

The students should describe their trains by naming the colors from left to right. Students will see that there are many correct answers for each of these commands. They can use the master on page 124 to record their answers by coloring their rod trains. The various answers to the same commands can be displayed on the bulletin board.

Trains are very important since they are the model for addition. This exercise should be kept light and fun. It helps students process verbal commands. It also helps develop creativity, as students are able to respond to each command with many correct answers. It helps them verbalize a visual situation as they name the colors, and gives them confidence as they make up commands for other students to follow.

Underlying Mathematics Related to the NCTM Standards:

Association of colors with rods
Meaning of addition
Comparisons of lengths
Counting
One-to-one correspondence
Communication and verbalization of ideas

Playing Challenge Match for Addends

Materials
Cuisenaire Rods for each pair of students

Settings
Two students working together
A small group, students working in pairs
A whole class, students working in pairs

Learning Experience

This Challenge Match Game provides motivating practice with trains in preparation for work with addition. When a two-car train is matched by a single rod, the three rods are called a *rod triple* or a *triple of rods*. For example:

To start the game, place 40–50 assorted rods in the center of the table for each pair of students. The first player chooses a rod (other than white) and challenges the second player to make a two-car train that matches it. The second player keeps the triple of rods once the match has been made. For example, if the challenge had been a black rod, one possible match would be the two-car train yellow + red.

Then the second player chooses a rod and challenges the first player to make a two-car train that matches it. The white rod can never be used as the challenge. The first player keeps the triple of rods once the match has been made. The players reverse roles again. The pile of rods in the center of the table gets smaller each time. The object of the game is to "stump your partner," by choosing a single rod for which no two-car train can be made from the rods left on the table. The player who makes the challenge that cannot be matched is the winner of the game and scores one point for each rod left on the table. Students should play this several times, since it helps them build readiness for work with addends. They will enjoy the game during their free time as well as during their mathematics class time.

Underlying Mathematics Related to the NCTM Standards:

Recognition of equivalences of lengths
Association of colors with lengths
Meaning of addition
Association of various addends for a sum

Use of the terms *rod triple* and *triple of rods*
Visual thinking
Reasoning and proof
Communication and verbalization of ideas

Materials

Cuisenaire Rods for each student
Crayons matching the rod colors for each student
Pencil for each student
Finding All Two-Car Trains:
Worksheet 1, page 125
Worksheet 2, page 126

Settings

One student working individually
A small group, students working individually
A small group, students working in pairs

Learning Experience

On the worksheets on pages 125 and 126, students intuitively find various pairs of addends for the same sum. They may find it helpful to use rods to build the two-car trains prior to coloring them on the worksheets.

In order to be sure that all trains have been found, students need to use a systematic approach. One approach is to build a train and then reverse the cars by means of the commutative property of addition. A second approach is to proceed by means of staircase patterns.

Other patterns are interesting in that the number of two-car trains is always one less than the length (in terms of white rods) of the rod being matched. For example, the red rod has 1 two-car train; the green rod has 2 two-car trains; the purple rod has 3 two-car trains; the yellow rod has 4 two-car trains, etc.

The addends for orange are particularly useful for laying groundwork for the addition of large numbers. For example, in adding 8 + 7, students will be taught that if you add 2 to 8, you get 10. Taking the 2 from the 7 leaves 5; hence, 8 + 7 = 10 + 5, or 15.

Solutions

Finding All Two-Car Trains Worksheet 1 (p. 125)
1) P = W + G
P = R + R
P = G + W
(in the order of staircase patterns)

2) D = W + Y
D = Y + W
D = P + R
D = R + P
D = G + G
(using the commutative property)

3) N = W + K
N = R + D
N = G + Y
N = P + P
N = Y + G
N = D + R
N = K + W
(in order of staircase patterns)

Finding All Two-Car Trains Worksheet 2   (p. 126)
1) E = W + N
E = N + W
E = R + K
E = K + R
E = G + D

E = D + G
E = P + Y
E = Y + P
(using the commutative property)

2) O = W + E
O = R + N
O = G + K
O = P + D
O = Y + Y
O = D + P
O = K + G
O = N + R
O = E + W
(in order of staircase patterns)

Underlying Mathematics Related to the NCTM Standards:

Recognition of equivalences of lengths
Association of three-dimensional rods and two-dimensional representations
Association of codes with rods
Association of various addends for a sum
Ordering lengths

Commutative property of addition
Patterns
Reasoning and proof
Communication and verbalization of findings

Introducing the Plus Sign

Materials
Cuisenaire Rods for each student

Settings
A small group led by the teacher
A whole class led by the teacher

Learning Experience

Ask students to make all the two-car trains for the purple rod and to describe each train in words.

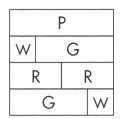

purple

white plus green

red plus red

green plus white

Now introduce the symbol "+" for "plus" and record each train with coding:

W + G
R + R
G + W

Ask students to make all the two-car trains for the yellow rod and to record each train with coding:

W + P
R + G
G + R
P + W

Write some plus stories on the board and have the students build the trains:

Y + G	R + K	E + W
K + R	D + R	P + Y
P + W	W + N	N + R

At this stage, students do not need to match each train with a single rod to find the sum.

Underlying Mathematics Related to the NCTM Standards:
Recognition of equivalences of lengths
Association of codes with rods
Association of rods with codes
Meaning of addition
Communication and verbalization of findings

Practicing the Plus Sign

Materials

Cuisenaire Rods for each student
Crayons matching the rod colors for each student
Pencil for each student
Practicing the Plus Sign:
    Worksheet 1, page 127
    Worksheet 2, page 128
    Worksheet 3, page 129
    Worksheet 4, page 130

Settings

One student working individually
A small group, students working individually
A whole class, students working individually

Learning Experience

This series of worksheets carefully develops the use of the plus sign, "+." On the worksheets on pages 127 and 128, students are given trains and are asked to write stories using codes. On the worksheets on pages 129 and 130, they are given the plus stories and are asked to color the trains to reinforce the association of codes and rods.

The use of coding need not be algebraic. Each code letter may be read as a color name and not the alphabet name. For example, D + P is read, "dark green plus purple." The purpose of the coding is to provide a shorthand way to share information in writing about the rods.

If a student is not ready for the coding, the concepts can be developed by means of concrete manipulation of rods, pictorial coloring exercises, and verbal communication of color names. For example, on the worksheets on pages 127 and 128, students can find the rods, color the pictures, and name the colors. On the worksheets on pages 129 and 130, the teacher can dictate the colors. Students can find rods and color the trains.

Students need not find the sums at this stage of development. Hence, plus stories with more than two cars can be given here. Finding sums will be restricted initially to two-car trains, but sums for trains with more than two cars will be considered starting on page 90.

Solutions

Practicing the Plus Sign Worksheet 1 (p. 127)
1) D + P
2) W + P
3) N + W
4) R + G + W
5) Y + G + R

Practicing the Plus Sign Worksheet 2 (p. 128)
1) G + G
2) N + R
3) D + P
4) Y + G
5) W + D
6) K + G

Practicing the Plus Sign Worksheet 3 (p. 129)	
1) green	3 squares
dark green	6 squares
2) blue	9 squares
white	1 square
3) red	2 squares
black	7 squares
4) yellow	5 squares
green	3 squares
5) dark green	6 squares
purple	4 squares

Practicing the Plus Sign Worksheet 4 (p.130)	
1) black	7 squares
red	2 squares
2) green	3 squares
purple	4 squares
3) brown	8 squares
white	1 square
4) dark green	6 squares
green	3 squares
5) red	2 squares
brown	8 squares
6) yellow	5 squares
yellow	5 squares

Underlying Mathematics Related to the NCTM Standards:
Association of codes with rods
Association of rods with codes
Meaning of addition
Use of plus sign
Counting
Reasoning and proof
Communication and verbalization of findings

Finding Lengths of Two-Car Trains

Materials
Cuisenaire Rods for each student

Settings
A small group led by the teacher
A whole class led by the teacher

Learning Experience
Ask students to place a red rod and a purple rod end to end.

R	P

Then ask students to find a one-car train that matches this two-car train. Some students may try several rods beside the two-car train before they find the single rod that matches exactly.

R	P
D	

Red plus purple equals dark green.

Provide students with several oral examples to solve, such as:

green plus yellow	[brown]
brown plus white	[blue]
red plus red	[purple]
purple plus dark green	[orange]
black plus white	[brown]
white plus dark green	[black]
green plus black	[orange]

At this stage of development, select examples so that the train length does not exceed the length of one orange rod.

Students will enjoy making problems for the class to solve. If any train exceeds the length of one orange rod, the answer can simply be given as "the sum is longer than orange." Work on trains longer than orange will be covered on pages 77–90.

Underlying Mathematics Related to the NCTM Standards:

Recognition of equivalences of lengths
Use of the terms *rod triple* and *triple of rods*
Meaning of addition
Use of the terms addend and sum

Association of sums with addends
Visual thinking
Reasoning and proof
Communication and verbalization of findings

Playing the Train Story Game

Materials
Cuisenaire Rods for each group
60 index cards for each group

Settings
A small group working together
A whole class working in small groups

Learning Experience
Make a deck of 60 cards, 6 cards for each of the 10 rod codes: W, R, G, P, Y, D, K, N, E, and O.

The cards are shuffled, and each player is dealt four cards. The rest of the cards are placed face down to form a stack in the center of the table. One card is turned face up to start a discard pile.

On a turn, a player takes either the top card from the discard pile or the top card from the stack. Using the rods to help, the player then tries to make a "book" of three cards: a two-car train and the appropriate single length for its sum.

For example:
If the player's cards were E, R, Y, N, and P, the player could make a book with Y, P, and E, since Y + P equals E.

The player should prove the plus story with the rods. If correct, the player puts the three cards that formed the book face down in front of himself and selects three more cards from the discard pile or stack.

Whenever a book cannot be made, the player discards one card face up on the discard pile, and it becomes the next player's turn. The game ends when the cards in the stack run out. The player with the most books wins.

Underlying Mathematics Related to the NCTM Standards:
Recognition of equivalences of lengths
Association of codes with rods
Association of rods with codes
Association of sums with addends
Meaning of addition
Reasoning and proof
Communication and verbalization of ideas

Varying the Train Story Game

Materials
Cuisenaire Rods for each group
60 index cards for each group

Settings
A small group working together
A whole class working in small groups

Learning Experience

Make a deck of 60 cards, 6 cards for each of the 10 rod codes: W, R, G, P, Y, D, K, N, E, and O.

The cards are shuffled and the top four cards are placed face up in the center of the table. Each player is dealt three cards face down. The deck is placed face down in the center of the table. The goal is to make "books" of three cards: a two-car train and the appropriate single car length for its sum. Each book is comprised of two cards from the player's hand and one from the center of the table.

For example:
Center of the Table: G, K, W, and E
Player's Hand: R, Y, and W
Since R + G equals Y, the player makes the book R, G, and Y.

The player should prove the plus story with the rods. If correct, the player keeps the three cards in the book. The two cards from his hand are replaced with two cards from the deck, and the player gets another turn.

Whenever a player cannot make a book, he places one card from his hand face up in the center of the table and draws a card from the deck. The game ends when the cards in the deck run out. The player with the most books wins.

Underlying Mathematics Related to the NCTM Standards:
Recognition of equivalences of lengths
Association of codes with rods
Association of rods with codes
Association of sums with addends
Reasoning and proof
Communication and verbalization of ideas

Introducing the Equal Sign

Materials

Cuisenaire Rods for each student

Settings

A small group led by the teacher
A whole class led by the teacher

Learning Experience

Ask students to build a two-car train with red and black and to find the single length that matches it.

R	K
E	

Now introduce the symbol "=" for "is equal to" or "equals."
R + K = E is read, "Red plus black equals blue."

Hold up various pairs of rods. Ask students to find the single length that matches and then to write the plus story. For example, hold up:

green and white   black and red
purple and yellow   yellow and yellow
red and brown   dark green and green

Students should verify their answers by showing the rod triples.

The purpose of this activity is to introduce the equal sign so that a complete plus story can be written. At this stage of development, select examples so that the train length does not exceed the length of one orange rod. Lengths beyond orange will be developed starting on page 77.

Underlying Mathematics Related to the NCTM Standards:

Recognition of equivalences of lengths
Association of codes with rods
Association of sums with addends
Use of plus sign
Use of equal sign
Meaning of addition
Reasoning and proof

Writing Plus Stories

Materials

Cuisenaire Rods for each student
Crayons matching the rod colors for each student
Pencil for each student
Writing Plus Stories:
   Worksheet 1, page 131
   Worksheet 2, page 132

Settings

One student working individually
A small group, students working individually
A whole class, students working individually

Learning Experience

Students are asked to do two tasks on the worksheets on pages 131 and 132. They are to find the sum (single rod length) and then record the plus story using codes and symbols. The concept being developed here is addition. Some students will be able to tell the colors of the rods by counting the number of white rods on the centimeter grid. Most students are able to match and color the single rod length. It is important for students to note that the same sum can result from different pairs of addends.

For students who may have trouble recording the results with codes, have them say the plus story; for example, "Green plus dark green equals blue." This is precisely how the symbols G + D = E should be read.

In matching the rods to the centimeter graph paper strips, students are building readiness for numerical sums. Later, the plus stories with rods will be interpreted as addition sentences with numbers, with the white rod being assigned the numerical value 1.

Solutions

Writing Plus Stories Worksheet 1 (p. 131)
1) black, red, blue   K + R = E
2) red, green, yellow   R + G = Y
3) purple, white, yellow   P + W = Y
4) green, black, orange   G + K = O

Writing Plus Stories Worksheet 2 (p. 132)
1) yellow, yellow, orange   Y + Y = O
2) green, red, yellow   G + R = Y
3) black, green, orange   K + G = O
4) green, purple, black   G + P = K
5) white, yellow, dark green W + Y = D
6) brown, red, orange   N + R = O

Underlying Mathematics Related to the NCTM Standards:

Recognition of equivalences of lengths
Association of codes with rods
Association of sums with addends
Meaning of addition
Use of plus sign
Use of equal sign

Completing Plus Stories

Materials

Cuisenaire Rods for each student
Crayons matching the rod colors for each student
Pencil for each student
Completing Plus Stories:
    Worksheet 1, page 133
    Worksheet 2, page 134

Settings

One student working individually
A small group, students working individually
A whole class, students working individually

Learning Experience

On the worksheets on pages 133 and 134, the problems are given in codes and the students must find the appropriate rods before proceeding. The meaning of "+" is reinforced as being "Make a Train."

The addition process is done at the concrete level of finding the single car length that matches the train. The recording process is done on a pictorial level when students color the plus stories and on an abstract level when they write the plus stories in codes.

The intermediate step of coloring the single length may become the final step if students are not ready to deal with the abstract symbols. They can say the colors in the plus stories rather than write the plus stories.

Solutions

Completing Plus Stories Worksheet 1 (p. 133)
1) brown, red, orange   N + R = O
2) green, yellow, brown   G + Y = N
3) purple, red, dark green   P + R = D
4) red, dark green, brown   R + D = N

Completing Plus Stories Worksheet 2 (p. 134)
1) yellow, purple, blue   Y + P = E
2) black, white, brown   K + W = N
3) green, dark green, blue   G + D = E
4) red, yellow, black   R + Y = K
5) red, brown, orange   R + N = O

Underlying Mathematics Related to the NCTM Standards:

Recognition of equivalences of lengths
Association of codes with rods
Association of sums with addends
Meaning of addition
Use of plus sign
Use of equal sign

Finding Plus Story Patterns

Materials

Cuisenaire Rods for each student
Crayons matching the rod colors for each student
Pencil for each student
Finding Plus Story Patterns:
    Worksheet 1, page 135
    Worksheet 2, page 136
1-cm Graph Paper Master, page 99

Settings

One student working individually
A small group, students working individually
A small group, students working in pairs

Learning Experience

The worksheets on pages 135 and 136 are very exciting to share in class discussion once the students have worked on them for a reasonable time. Answers will be given in various orders, depending on how a student approaches the problem. For the larger rods, the possibilities are many, and it is not expected that an individual student find all the possible trains. Listing on the board the various trains that they find will yield a good sampling. If they are recorded in lists according to the number of cars in each train, students will develop better strategies for solving additional problems like this.

Students will enjoy coloring these designs, as the patterns look like Navaho rugs. The designs for other rods can be colored on centimeter graph paper, using the master on page 99.

This activity leads to many mathematical patterns. For example, the total number of trains for each successive rod are powers of 2. The white rod has 1 possible train; the red rod has 2 possible trains; the green rod has 4 possible trains; the purple rod has 8 possible trains; the yellow rod has 16 possible trains; the dark green rod has 32 possible trains; the black rod has 64 possible trains; the brown rod has 128 possible trains; the blue rod has 256 possible trains; and the orange rod has 512 possible trains. It is helpful for students to sort the trains according to the number of cars.

Solutions

Finding Plus Story Patterns Worksheet 1 (p. 135)
There are 8 possible trains for purple:

one-car train	two-car trains	three-car trains	four-car train
P = P	W + G = P	W + W + R = P	W + W + W + W = P
	G + W = P	W + R + W = P	
	R + R = P	R + W + W = P	

Finding Plus Story Patterns Worksheet 2 (p. 136)
There are 512 possible trains for orange. A way to organize them is by the number of cars, from one to ten.

one-car train	two-car trains	three-car trains	up to	ten-car train
O = O	W + E = O	W + W + N = O		W + W + W + W +
	R + N = O	W + R + K = O		W + W + W + W +
	G + K = O	W + G + D = O		W + W = O
	etc.	etc.		

Underlying Mathematics Related to the NCTM Standards:

Recognition of equivalences of lengths
Association of codes with rods
Association of various addends for a sum
Patterns
Problem solving
Communication and verbalization of ideas

Changing the Order

Materials

Cuisenaire Rods for each student
Crayons matching the rod colors
Pencil for each student
Changing the Order Worksheet, page 137

Settings

One student working individually
A small group, students working individually
A whole class, students working individually

Learning Experience

The worksheet on page 137 allows students to reinforce the commutative property of addition. Although the two trains are in a different order, they match the same single rod length. Students should conclude that the order of the cars does not affect the total length.

The commutative property is especially important as a concept as students begin to learn the basic facts of addition. It permits the student to learn only half the addition facts. For example, if a student knows 3 + 1, the commutative property says that 1 + 3 will have the same answer.

Problems can also be made easier by changing the order of the addends. For example, 2 + 9 will give the same sum as 9 + 2. It is shorter to start with 9 and count 2 more (10, 11) than to start with 2 and count 9 more (3, 4, 5, 6, 7, 8, 9, 10, 11).

The word *commutative* should be related to the term *commute*, meaning to exchange places.

Solutions

Changing the Order Worksheet (p. 137)
1) purple, white, yellow   P + W = Y; W + P = Y
2) yellow, green, brown   Y + G = N; G + Y = N
3) brown, red, orange   N + R = O; R + N = O

Underlying Mathematics Related to the NCTM Standards:
Recognition of equivalences of lengths
Association of codes with rods
Association of sums with addends
Commutative property of addition
Patterns
Reasoning and proof
Communication and verbalization of ideas

Using the Same Three Rods

Materials
Cuisenaire Rods for each student
Pencil for each student
Using the Same Three Rods Worksheet, page 138
Crayons matching the rod colors (optional)

Settings
One student working individually
A small group, students working individually
A whole class, students working individually

Learning Experience

Students are not expected to use rods in this activity. Knowing that changing the order of two rods in a train does not change the total length, students should simply rewrite the problem to indicate the change in order. The three rods—known as a *rod triple* or a *triple of rods*—can generate two different plus stories, depending on the order of the rods in the two-car train.

If students do not seem convinced about the commutative property of addition, ask them to build the train described by their new plus story and to verify that it matches the given plus story.

Students may color the rods if they wish. The main purpose of this sheet is the abstract manipulation of the symbols according to the commutative property of addition.

Solutions

Using the Same Three Rods Worksheet (p. 138)
1) W + R = G
2) R + D = N
3) N + W = E
4) K + G = O

Underlying Mathematics Related to the NCTM Standards:
Recognition of equivalences of lengths
Association of various addends for a sum
Commutative property of addition
Patterns
Use of the terms *rod triple* and *triple of rods*
Reasoning and proof
Communication and verbalization of ideas

Changing Rod Stories to Number Sentences

Materials

Cuisenaire Rods for each student
Paper and pencil for each student
Changing Rod Stories to Number Sentences
   Worksheet, page 139

Settings

A small group led by the teacher
A whole class led by the teacher

Learning Experience

Ask students to make a train with a red rod and a green rod. Ask them to find the single rod that matches and to write the plus story for the rod triple.

R + G = Y

Direct students to cover each rod with white rods. Now ask them to describe the rod situation in terms of white rods:
"2 white rods plus 3 white rods equals 5 white rods."

This rod triple can be written in an addition sentence with numerals, assuming a white rod represents 1.

2 + 3 = 5

The distinction is made in this development between a plus story, which describes the situation with rods, and a number sentence, which uses numerals to interpret the rod lengths in terms of white rods.

The worksheet on page 139 gives students practice going from a rod story to a number sentence. Coloring the rod lengths on the centimeter strips reinforces the relationship of each rod length to white rods.

Solutions

Changing Rod Stories to Number Sentences Worksheet (p. 139)
1) green, red, yellow   3 + 2 = 5
2) dark green, green, blue   6 + 3 = 9
3) brown, white, blue   8 + 1 = 9
4) black, green, orange   7 + 3 = 10
5) white, blue, orange   1 + 9 = 10
6) purple, purple, brown   4 + 4 = 8

Underlying Mathematics Related to the NCTM Standards:

Recognition of equivalences of lengths
Representation of lengths in terms of white rods
Association of sums with addends
Association of numbers with rods
Use of equal sign
Meaning of addition
Use of addition sentences
Use of the terms *rod triple* and *triple of rods*

Writing Addition Sentences

Materials

Cuisenaire Rods for each student
Crayons matching the rod colors for each student
Pencil for each student
Writing Addition Sentences:
   Worksheet 1, page 140
   Worksheet 2, page 141

Settings

One student working individually
A small group, students working individually
A whole class, students working individually

Learning Experience

The worksheets on pages 140 and 141 mark the beginning of an extension to more traditional arithmetic work. On these worksheets, students carefully proceed through all the developmental stages for the concept of addition. Students work at the concrete level, manipulating rods to find the sum; think at the pictorial level by coloring pictures of the rods; and then proceed to the numerical level of writing addition sentences with numerals.

The strip of centimeter graph paper will make the transition from rods to numerals more apparent, since each grid is the length of one white rod. Hence, the arithmetic computation is a mere recording of a physical situation. The length of each rod involved in the addition process is expressed in terms of white rods.

Solutions

Writing Addition Sentences Worksheet 1 (p. 140)
1) green, green, dark green $3 + 3 = 6$
2) yellow, green, brown $5 + 3 = 8$
3) purple, red, dark green $4 + 2 = 6$
4) yellow, yellow, orange $5 + 5 = 10$
5) black, red, blue $7 + 2 = 9$

Writing Addition Sentences Worksheet 2 (p. 141)
Note: The last two problems demonstrate the commutative property of addition.
1) green, red, yellow $3 + 2 = 5$
2) black, green, orange $7 + 3 = 10$
3) white, dark green, black $1 + 6 = 7$
4) purple, yellow, blue $4 + 5 = 9$
5) dark green, purple, orange $6 + 4 = 10$
6) purple, dark green, orange $4 + 6 = 10$

<u>Underlying Mathematics Related to the NCTM Standards:</u>
Recognition of equivalences of lengths
Representation of lengths in terms of white rods
Association of sums with addends
Use of equal sign
Meaning of addition
Use of addition sentences
Commutative property of addition

Practicing Addition Sentences

Materials

Cuisenaire Rods for each student
Crayons matching the rod colors for each student
Pencil for each student
Practicing Addition Sentences:
    Worksheet 1, page 142
    Worksheet 2, page 143
    Master, page 144

Settings

One student working individually
A small group, students working individually
A whole class, students working individually

Learning Experience

On the worksheets on pages 142 and 143, each plus story is interpreted as a train to be colored on the top strip of graph paper. The sum is colored on the bottom strip. A transition is being made from the pictorial level to the abstract level. However, students may work at the concrete level with actual rods if they wish.

The conversion to numerals comes from relating each rod to a matching number of white rods. The addition sentences are written with numerals. At this stage of development, the sums should be kept less than or equal to the length of one orange rod (10 white rods).

This learning experience is an important transition point from rods to numerals, so many practice opportunities are warranted. The master on page 144 allows the students or teacher to write additional plus stories. It should be noted that this type of master could be used following page 80 for sums through 20 by making the centimeter grids 20 cm long.

Solutions

Practicing Addition Sentences Worksheet 1 (p. 142)
1) white, yellow, dark green $1 + 5 = 6$
2) dark green, red, brown $6 + 2 = 8$
3) green, green, dark green $3 + 3 = 6$
4) purple, dark green, orange $4 + 6 = 10$

Practicing Addition Sentences Worksheet 2 (p. 143)
1) green, red, yellow $3 + 2 = 5$
2) yellow, purple, blue $5 + 4 = 9$
3) red, white, green $2 + 1 = 3$
4) purple, dark green, orange $4 + 6 = 10$
5) black, red, blue $7 + 2 = 9$

Underlying Mathematics Related to the NCTM Standards:
Recognition of equivalences of lengths
Representation of lengths in terms of white rods
Association of sums with addends
Use of equal sign
Meaning of addition
Use of addition sentences

Finding Sums

Materials

Cuisenaire Rods for each student
Crayons matching the rod colors for each student
Pencil for each student
Finding Sums:
Worksheet 1, page 145
Worksheet 2, page 146
Master, page 147

Settings

One student working individually
A small group, students working individually
A whole class, students working individually

Learning Experience

The purpose of the worksheets on pages 145 and 146 is to relate numerals to the physical model provided by the rods. The ultimate use of the model is to provide a method for translating abstract symbols of mathematics into concrete representations. For a student, the concrete manipulation is eventually replaced by a mental visualization of that manipulation or by a pictorial representation of it.

It is important to go from numerals to rods, and from rods to numerals, to reinforce the addition facts being developed. Students start to visualize the meaning of 2 + 3 equals 5.

Repeated practice on worksheets like these is warranted. Hence, the master on page 147 is left open-ended so that further problems can be posed by the students or by the teacher.

Solutions

Finding Sums Worksheet 1 (p. 145)
1) yellow, purple, blue   5 + 4 = 9
2) white, black, brown   1 + 7 = 8
3) green, dark green, blue   3 + 6 = 9
4) brown, red, orange   8 + 2 = 10
5) dark green, purple, orange   6 + 4 = 10

Finding Sums Worksheet 2 (p. 146)
1) green, purple, black   3 + 4 = 7
2) yellow, yellow, orange   5 + 5 = 10
3) purple, white, yellow   4 + 1 = 5
4) red, dark green, brown   2 + 6 = 8
5) yellow, red, black   5 + 2 = 7
6) black, green, orange   7 + 3 = 10

Underlying Mathematics Related to the NCTM Standards:

Recognition of equivalences of lengths
Representation of lengths in terms of white rods
Association of sums with addends
Association of numbers with rods

Use of equal sign
Meaning of addition
Use of addition sentences
Reasoning and proof

Using a Number Line to Add

Materials

Cuisenaire Rods for each student
Pencil for each student
Using a Number Line to Add:
Worksheet 1, page 148
Worksheet 2, page 149
Master, page 150

Settings

One student working individually
A small group, students working individually
A whole class, students working individually

Learning Experience

The placement of rods on a number line marked in centimeters is another method of representing numbers with the rods. Again, the length of a white rod serves as a useful unit for the whole number work with addition.

A rod represents the first addend with its left edge at 0. The second addend is placed so that the rods are end to end. The total length can be read directly from the number line.

The worksheets on pages 148 and 149 use the number line approach to provide a visualization of the abstract processes. The master on page 150 is open-ended for further practice as needed.

Solutions

Using a Number Line to Add Worksheet 1 (p. 148)
1) red, purple   2 + 4 = 6
2) dark green, red   6 + 2 = 8
3) yellow, green   5 + 3 = 8
4) purple, yellow   4 + 5 = 9
5) white, blue   1 + 9 = 10
6) red, black   2 + 7 = 9
7) black, green   7 + 3 = 10

Using a Number Line to Add Worksheet 2 (p. 149)
1) red, yellow   2 + 5 = 7
2) yellow, green   5 + 3 = 8
3) black, red   7 + 2 = 9
4) purple, purple   4 + 4 = 8
5) white, dark green 1 + 6 = 7
6) green, purple   3 + 4 = 7
7) dark green, green 6 + 3 = 9
8) blue, white   9 + 1 = 10
9) red, brown   2 + 8 = 10

Underlying Mathematics Related to the NCTM Standards:

Recognition of equivalences of lengths
Representation of lengths in terms of white rods
Association of sums with addends
Association of numbers with rods
Use of equal sign
Meaning of addition
Use of addition sentences

Building an Addition Table for Sums Through 10

Materials
Cuisenaire Rods for each student
Pencil for each student
Building an Addition Table for Sums Through 10
  Worksheet, page 151

Settings
One student working individually
A small group, students working individually
A small group, students working in pairs

Learning Experience

An addition table is a very compact way of showing the addition facts. The two tables shown on the worksheet deal only with facts in which the sum is less than or equal to the length of one orange rod (10 white rods).

When the first table is completed, it looks like a city with skyscrapers of ascending and descending heights. The rod for each sum is stood on end in the appropriate square of the table. The solutions below show the code for each rod to be stood on end. Some students may not have the fine motor control to complete the task without the rods toppling over. These students can do only the left corner of the table going from W to Y, or they can simply write the codes for the sums in the appropriate squares.

The second table can be completed by those students who are able to write the numerals. It can also be done as a group project to produce a larger copy that can be posted on the bulletin board for students to observe on a regular basis.

The tables show many patterns. These should be shared and discussed. Some important patterns include:
- The entries in each row (column) increase by one white rod, as in a staircase.
- The corresponding rows and columns have identical entries because of the commutative property of addition.
- Constant sums lie on diagonals going from the top right to the bottom left.

Solutions

Building an Addition Table for Sums Through 10 Worksheet (p. 151)

+	W	R	G	P	Y	D	K	N	E
W	R	G	P	Y	D	K	N	E	O
R	G	P	Y	D	K	N	E	O	
G	P	Y	D	K	N	E	O		
P	Y	D	K	N	E	O			
Y	D	K	N	E	O				
D	K	N	E	O					
K	N	E	O						
N	E	O							
E	O								

+	1	2	3	4	5	6	7	8	9
1	2	3	4	5	6	7	8	9	10
2	3	4	5	6	7	8	9	10	
3	4	5	6	7	8	9	10		
4	5	6	7	8	9	10			
5	6	7	8	9	10				
6	7	8	9	10					
7	8	9	10						
8	9	10							
9	10								

Underlying Mathematics Related to the NCTM Standards:
Representation of lengths in terms of white rods
Association of sums with addends
Association of numbers with rods
Use of table with rows and columns

Meaning of addition
Commutative property of addition
Patterns
Communication and verbalization of ideas

Checking Sums Through 10

Materials

Cuisenaire Rods for each student
Pencil for each student
Checking Sums Through 10:
   Worksheet 1, page 152
   Worksheet 2, page 153

Settings

One student working individually
A small group, students working individually
A whole class, students working individually

Learning Experience

The worksheets on pages 152 and 153 provide, in a traditional format, addition problems whose sums are less than or equal to 10. Students should be encouraged to interpret each problem with rods and to think through the solution in their heads on an abstract level. When the worksheets are completed, students can check their answers with the rods.

If some students are still operating on a concrete level, they should use the rods to help find sums using the number line provided at the bottom of each worksheet. The rods may not be needed for all the problems; students will know some of the facts more easily than others. They also should be

encouraged to use known facts to help figure out unknown facts. Students should also observe that the same sum could result from different pairs of addends. However, a given pair of addends has a unique answer as a sum.

The last two problems on both worksheets involve zero as an addend. This zero should be interpreted as the absence of rods. For example, 4 + 0 means a train of purple and no other rod; hence, the total length is purple. When zero is added to a number, the result is the number itself. In mathematics, zero is called the identity element for addition.

Solutions

Checking Sums Through 10 Worksheet 1 (p. 152)

1) green, yellow	8	**10)** purple, purple	8
2) dark green, green	9	**11)** red, brown	10
3) white, black	8	**12)** dark green, white	7
4) purple, green	7	**13)** green, green	6
5) red, red	4	**14)** yellow, purple	9
6) red, green	5	**15)** dark green, purple	10
7) yellow, yellow	10	**16)** black, red	9
8) white, red	3	**17)** purple, no rod	4
9) green, black	10	**18)** no rod, blue	9

Checking Sums Through 10 Worksheet 2 (p. 153)

1) red, purple	6	**10)** green, dark green	9
2) white, green	4	**11)** green, purple	7
3) green, red	5	**12)** red, dark green	8
4) purple, red	6	**13)** brown, red	10
5) purple, white	5	**14)** yellow, yellow	10
6) white, purple	5	**15)** purple, dark green	10
7) white, dark green	7	**16)** blue, white	10
8) white, brown	9	**17)** green, no rod	3
9) red, yellow	7	**18)** no rod, black	7

Underlying Mathematics Related to the NCTM Standards:

Association of sums with addends
Association of numbers with rods
Concept of zero
Meaning of addition
Zero as an addend
Reasoning and proof

Wishing for a Longer Rod

Materials
Cuisenaire Rods for each student
Cuisenaire Rods for the teacher
Empty box or can (optional)

Settings
A small group led by the teacher
A whole class led by the teacher

Learning Experience

Take a green rod in your hand. Tell the students:
I have a green rod.
I WISH I HAD a brown rod.
Find the rod I need to make the train as long as the brown rod.

Some students will need to try several rods before finding the correct answer. By trial and error, students can see that some rods are too long; some are too short; but one is "just right," namely, the yellow rod.

Play "I WISH I HAD" for other rods. Do this activity many times; let a student act as leader to tell the "I WISH I HAD" story. A "silent" version of the game can also be played by establishing ahead of time one rod as the WISH for a whole series of problems. The leader holds up one rod at a time; the other students hold up the rod that combines with the leader's rod to give the "wished for" length.

The fantasy of wishing is very motivating for students. It is also possible to decorate a box or can with crepe paper to make a wishing well. One student acts as a leader and tosses a rod into the well, while making a wish for a longer rod. Another student comes up with the missing addend and checks the results by completing the rod train.

Underlying Mathematics Related to the NCTM Standards:
Recognition of equivalences of lengths
Missing addends
Meaning of subtraction
Connections between missing addends and subtraction
Reasoning and proof
Communication and verbalization of ideas

Playing Challenge Match for Missing Addends

Materials

Cuisenaire Rods for each pair of students

Settings

Two students working together
A small group, students working in pairs
A whole class, students working in pairs

Learning Experience

Place 40–50 assorted rods in the center of the table for each pair of students. The first player chooses two rods of different colors and places them side by side. The second player must find the missing addend—the rod that will combine with the shorter rod to match the longer rod. For example, suppose a black rod and a green rod are given. The player must think: green plus what gives black.

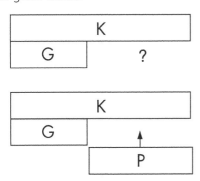

The answer will be a purple rod.

The second player keeps the three rods involved in the match. The partners then reverse roles. As the game continues, the pile of rods in the center of the table will get smaller and smaller. The object of the game is to make a challenge that cannot be matched with the remaining rods. The player to do this first wins the game and scores one point for each rod left in the center of the table. Score may be accumulated from game to game.

This game is enjoyable for students to play during free time and need not be played during scheduled mathematics class. Students may wish to alternate this version of Challenge Match with the Challenge Match for Addends game, described on page 42.

Underlying Mathematics Related to the NCTM Standards:

Awareness of rod attributes (length, color, and shape)
Association of colors with lengths
Recognition of equivalences of lengths
Missing addends
Meaning of subtraction
Connections between missing addends and subtraction
Reasoning and proof
Communication and verbalization of ideas

Solving the Case of the Missing Addend

Materials

Cuisenaire Rods for each student
An orange rod for each student
Orange construction paper for each pair of students
Dark green, black, brown, and blue
    construction paper (optional)

Settings

A small group, students working in pairs
A whole class, students working in pairs

Learning Experience

Each student should make an orange rod case out of a piece of orange construction paper. The orange construction paper should be cut the exact length of an orange rod (10 cm), with a width of about 5 cm. Then it is wrapped around an orange rod and taped together in order to make a loose-fitting case the length of an orange rod. Then the orange rod should be removed from the case and placed in the center of the table to serve as a frame of reference.

Without letting the second player see, the first player fills the rod case exactly with two rods (a two-car train for orange). The first player then shows the second player one end of the rod case. The second player interprets the situation using rods. The second player guesses the other rod in the rod case. The answer is checked by showing the other end of the rod case. For example, if dark green were showing at one end, purple would be showing on the other end.

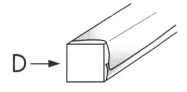

The partners switch roles. The player filling the rod case has to think about missing addends as much as the player guessing. Both players will find this activity fun and challenging. It is a very worthwhile activity since it stresses how much more is needed to make 10. If students are adding 9 + 6, knowing that 1 more is needed to make 10 helps them see that 9 + 6 can be thought of as 10 + 5, or 15. The "building to 10" technique is more efficient than the "counting on" method for sums beyond 10.

A more difficult version involving three addends is to make a "rod sandwich." Without letting the second player see, the first player fills the rod case exactly with three rods (a three-car train for orange). The first player shows the second player the two ends of the rod case. The second player has to name the rod in the middle (the "filling" in the sandwich). The answer is checked, and then the partners switch roles.

Students enjoy making rod cases for other rods, using the correct color of construction paper, and cutting the correct length. Especially useful are cases for dark green, black, brown, and blue. These give practice with addends for 6, 7, 8, and 9, respectively.

Underlying Mathematics Related to the NCTM Standards:
Recognition of equivalences of lengths
Missing addends
Visual memory of shapes
Connections between missing addends and subtraction
Reasoning and proof
Communication and verbalization of ideas

Practicing Missing Addends

Materials

Cuisenaire Rods for each student
Crayons matching the rod colors for each student
Pencil for each student
Practicing Missing Addends:
   Worksheet 1, page 154
   Worksheet 2, page 155
   Worksheet 3, page 156

Settings

One student working individually
A small group, students working individually
A whole class, students working individually

Learning Experience

The worksheets on pages 154–156 provide the pictorial stage in the development of the concept of missing addends. The games and activities on pages 62–64 are prerequisite to these worksheets.

On the worksheet on page 154, students are asked to draw and color the completed picture. It is important that the correct colors are used. Most likely, students will use the rods to find the answers. It is not important that the coloring of the missing rod be done beautifully. Students may outline the rod length first and then color in the picture.

The worksheet on page 155 is similar to the worksheet on page 154, but requires a further step of students writing the rod story.

On the worksheet on page 156, students need to respond to a missing rod story, find rods, color them on the strips, translate the story into numbers, color the missing rod length, and write the completed number sentence.

It should be noted that most students at this stage of development think of a missing addend situation as a missing piece in an addition problem. It is more sophisticated to realize that a subtraction technique (to be developed starting on page 68) can be used to find the missing length.

Solutions

Practicing Missing Addends Worksheet 1 (p. 154)
1) green
2) green
3) white
4) dark green
5) purple

Practicing Missing Addends Worksheet 2 (p. 155)
1) orange, white	W + ___ = O	W + E = O
2) yellow, red	R + ___ = Y	R + G = Y
3) black, green	G + ___ = K	G + P = K
4) brown, dark green	D + ___ = N	D + R = N
5) orange, brown	N + ___ = O	N + R = O
6) yellow, blue	Y + ___ = E	Y + P = E

Practicing Missing Addends Worksheet 3 (p. 156)
1) red, brown, orange	2 + ___ = 10	2 + 8 = 10
2) black, red, blue	7 + ___ = 9	7 + 2 = 9
3) purple, purple, brown	4 + ___ = 8	4 + 4 = 8
4) white, yellow, dark green	1 + ___ = 6	1 + 5 = 6
5) purple, green, black	4 + ___ = 7	4 + 3 = 7

Underlying Mathematics Related to the NCTM Standards:

Recognition of equivalences of lengths
Representation of lengths in terms of white rods
Missing addends
Use of addition sentences
Visual memory of shapes
Connections between missing addends and subtraction
Reasoning and proof
Communication and verbalization of ideas

Completing Missing Addend Sentences

Materials

Cuisenaire Rods for each student
Crayons matching the rod colors for each student
Pencil for each student
Completing Missing Addend Sentences:
> Worksheet 1, page 157
> Worksheet 2, page 158
> Worksheet 3, page 159

Settings

One student working individually
A small group, students working individually
A whole class, students working individually

Learning Experience

On the worksheets on pages 157 and 158, the numerical situation involving missing addends is interpreted with rods. Each numeral is thought to describe the number of white rods that match the particular rod. The rod described by each numeral is colored. Students find and color the missing rod, and then write the complete addition sentence.

The worksheet on page 159 should be done without using rods. The rods should be used to check answers rather than to derive answers. However, some students may need to place rods on the centimeter graph paper grid at the bottom of the worksheet to help them think through some of the more difficult problems. The last two examples bring up the notion of zero as an addend again, modeled by no rod in a train.

The work on missing addends is important to the next two major developments in this book: the concept of subtraction (as described on page 67) and the extension of one-digit addition to sums beyond ten (as described on page 80).

Solutions

Completing Missing Addend Sentences Worksheet 1 (p. 157)
1) yellow, yellow, orange   5 + 5 = 10
2) red, purple, dark green   2 + 4 = 6
3) white, blue, orange   1 + 9 = 10
4) green, yellow, brown   3 + 5 = 8
5) dark green, green, blue   6 + 3 = 9
6) red, yellow, black   2 + 5 = 7

Completing Missing Addend Sentences Worksheet 2 (p. 158)
1) red, dark green, brown   2 + 6 = 8
2) yellow, red, black   5 + 2 = 7
3) white, blue, orange   1 + 9 = 10
4) black, red, blue   7 + 2 = 9
5) green, green, dark green   3 + 3 = 6
6) yellow, green, brown   5 + 3 = 8
7) purple, dark green, orange   4 + 6 = 10

Completing Missing Addend Sentences Worksheet 3 (p. 159)
1) 6   9) 4
2) 1   10) 2
3) 5   11) 1
4) 2   12) 5
5) 1   13) 7
6) 7   14) 4
7) 5   15) 0
8) 7   16) 8

Underlying Mathematics Related to the NCTM Standards:

Recognition of equivalences of lengths
Representation of lengths in terms of white rods
Missing addends
Use of addition sentences
Visual memory of shapes

Connections between missing addends and subtraction
Concept of zero
Zero as an addend
Reasoning and proof

Subtracting by Finding How Much More

Materials
Cuisenaire Rods for each student
Cuisenaire Rods for the teacher

Settings
A small group led by the teacher
A whole class led by the teacher

Learning Experience

Ask students to choose a dark green rod and a red rod. Direct their attention to the difference in lengths of the two rods. How much more is the dark green rod than the red rod?

Students must find a rod that will combine with the red rod to make the length of the dark green rod.

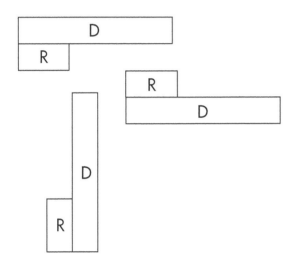

Any of these arrangements can be used to show that the purple rod exactly fits. While addition is shown by placing rods end to end, subtraction is shown by placing rods side by side.

Most students will sense that this way of viewing subtraction is similar to their work with missing addends. The rod configurations remain the same. All that has changed is the way of asking the question. The emphasis now is on the difference in length of two rods.

Do several more examples using the rods:

- *How much more is a black rod than a green rod?* [purple]
- *How much more is a blue rod than a purple rod?* [yellow]
- *How much more is an orange rod than a blue rod?* [white]
- *How much more is a dark green rod than a green rod?* [green]

Let students make up problems like these for their classmates to solve. It is important for students to verbalize the concepts in the form of questions to be interpreted with rods.

Underlying Mathematics Related to the NCTM Standards:
Recognition of equivalences of lengths
Missing addends
Meaning of subtraction
Visual memory of shapes
Connections between missing addends and subtraction
Reasoning and proof
Communication and verbalization of ideas

Teaching Subtraction as Take Away

Materials
Cuisenaire Rods for each student
Cuisenaire Rods for the teacher

Settings
A small group led by the teacher
A whole class led by the teacher

Learning Experience

Choose two rods; for example, a brown rod and a green rod. Ask students to imagine that an amount equal to the green rod is "taken away" or "cut off" from the brown rod. This can be demonstrated by placing the green rod on top of or below the brown rod so that the portion of the brown rod showing can be matched by a yellow rod.

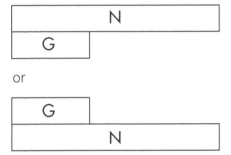

or

Brown "take away" green equals yellow.

Try more "take away" problems:
dark green "take away" red	[purple]
purple "take away" white	[green]
orange "take away" brown	[red]
blue "take away" yellow	[purple]
black "take away" white	[dark green]

After this activity, students will have experienced three views of subtraction, shown by placing rods side by side:
- as missing addends
- as "how much more" or "how many more" comparisons
- as "take away"

It is helpful to have more than one way to approach the concept of subtraction in order to meet individual differences and provide reinforcement. Also, word problems are stated in these three contexts, for example:

John has 2 pencils and José has 8 pencils. How many more pencils does John need to have the same number of pencils as José? (missing addend)

John has 2 pencils and José has 8 pencils. How many more pencils does José have than John? ("how many more" comparison)

José had 8 pencils and he gave John 2 of them. How many pencils does José have left? (take away)

The first two examples are harder for students because they contain the word "more," which is often associated with the operation of addition. The rods give very helpful practice with all three contexts for subtraction.

Underlying Mathematics Related to the NCTM Standards:
Recognition of equivalences of lengths
Missing addends
Meaning of subtraction
Connections between missing addends and subtraction
Reasoning and proof
Communication and verbalization of ideas

Finding the Difference

Materials

Cuisenaire Rods for each student
Crayons matching the rod colors for each student
Finding the Difference:
    Worksheet, page 160
    Master, page 161
Cuisenaire Rods for the overhead (optional)

Settings

A small group led by the teacher
A whole class led by the teacher

Learning Experience

The worksheet on page 160 gives pictorial practice on finding the difference between two rods. Students may use the rods if they need to. The learning experiences on pages 66–68 are prerequisite to this worksheet since the concept of subtraction using rods should be well established before entering this pictorial stage. This worksheet lends itself nicely to use of the transparent Cuisenaire Rods for the overhead projector.

The master on page 161 has been left open-ended so that the teacher can give problems orally. Describe each of the following "take away" situations orally. The students should color the appropriate rods on the graph paper strips provided and find the missing length.

orange "take away" red	[brown]
purple "take away" green	[white]
brown "take away" yellow	[green]
black "take away" white	[dark green]
blue "take away" dark green	[green]

Students may need many more practice opportunities to establish the concept, so this master may be used several times.

Solutions

Finding the Difference Worksheet (p. 160)
1) yellow, red, green
2) brown, purple, purple
3) blue, green, dark green
4) dark green, green, green
5) orange, white, blue

Underlying Mathematics Related to the NCTM Standards:

Recognition of equivalences of lengths
Missing addends
Meaning of subtraction
Representation of lengths in terms of white rods
Connections between missing addends and subtraction
Reasoning and proof
Communication and verbalization of ideas

Playing the Subtraction Game

Materials

Cuisenaire Rods for each pair of students
Empty container for each student

Settings

A small group, students working in pairs
A whole class, students working in pairs

Learning Experience

Place 40–50 rods in the center of the table to be used for scoring. Provide each pair of students with 40–50 rods to be used in playing the game. Ask partners to share their rods so that each student has the same number of rods of each color. The students put their rods into their empty containers and hold them under the table, out of view.

One student counts to three. On the count of three, each student takes one rod from the container and puts it on the table. The two rods are compared. The player with the longer rod wins. The score is the difference between the two rods. A rod equal to the difference is taken from the scoring rods and kept by the winning player. The two rods involved in the subtraction are discarded.

It should be noted that if the two rods to be subtracted are the same color, the score is zero. This is a subtle way of introducing the concept of zero, which occurs when a number is subtracted from itself.

The game ends when all the rods in the containers have been used. Each partner makes a train of his or her scoring rods. The player with the longer train wins the game.

Underlying Mathematics Related to the NCTM Standards:

One-to-one correspondence
Recognition of equivalences of lengths
Meaning of subtraction
Missing addends

Inequality and equality
Concept of zero
Connections between missing addends and subtraction
Communication and verbalization of ideas

Materials

Cuisenaire Rods for each student
Cuisenaire Rods for the teacher
Paper and pencil for each student

Settings

A small group led by the teacher
A whole class led by the teacher

Learning Experience

Ask students to take an orange rod and a green rod and to build a subtraction situation by putting the rods side by side.

Introduce the minus sign, "−," for subtraction.

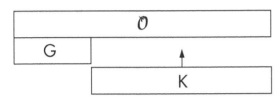

O − G = K is "Orange minus green equals black."

Ask students to interpret and solve these subtraction sentences:

Y − R = ?   E − P = ?   D − W = ?

An interesting exercise for students is to take three rods, such as red, yellow, and black, and to form all the possible addition and subtraction sentences for the three rods. For example:

R + Y = K	K = R + Y	K − R = Y
Y = K − R	Y + R = K	K = Y + R
K − Y = R	R = K − Y	

Choose other triples of rods and ask students to form all the possible addition and subtraction situations with the three rods. This type of activity will be done with numbers on page 76.

Underlying Mathematics Related to the NCTM Standards:

Recognition of equivalences of lengths
Association of codes with rods
Missing addends
Meaning of subtraction
Use of minus sign

Connections between missing addends and subtraction
Use of the terms *rod triple* and *triple of rods*
Reasoning and proof
Communication and verbalization of ideas

Recording Minus Stories

Materials
Cuisenaire Rods for each student
Crayons matching the rod colors (optional)
Pencil for each student
Recording Minus Stories:
  Worksheet 1, page 162
  Worksheet 2, page 163
  Master, page 164

Settings
One student working individually
A small group, students working individually
A whole class, students working individually

Learning Experience
On the worksheet on page 162, students need to match the pictures with rods and translate the subtraction situation of rods side by side into a minus story. The differences are not found. The intent of this worksheet is practice with the minus sign. It should be noted that the same rod configurations also could have been interpreted in terms of missing addends. For example, P + ___ = D describes the same situation as D – P = ___. This illustrates the close relationship between addition and subtraction as inverse operations.

The worksheet on page 163 requires both the initial minus story given by the rods and then the completed minus story. Students may wish to color the missing rod length or simply shade it in with pencil.

The master on page 164 is open-ended so that more problems may be posed by the students or by the teacher.

Solutions

Recording Minus Stories Worksheet 1 (p. 162)
1) O – K
2) Y – R
3) R – W
4) N – Y

Recording Minus Stories Worksheet 2 (p. 163)
1) Y – P   Y – P = W
2) G – R   G – R = W
3) K – P   K – P = G
4) O – K   O – K = G
5) O – D   O – D = P

Underlying Mathematics Related to the NCTM Standards:

Recognition of equivalences of lengths
Association of codes with rods
Meaning of subtraction
Use of minus sign

Missing addends
Connections between missing addends and subtraction
Reasoning and proof
Communication and verbalization of ideas

Writing Subtraction Sentences

Materials

Cuisenaire Rods for each student
Crayons matching the rod colors for each student
Pencil for each student
Writing Subtraction Sentences:
Worksheet 1, page 165
Worksheet 2, page 166
Master, page 167

Settings

One student working individually
A small group, students working individually
A whole class, students working individually

Learning Experience

On the worksheets on pages 165 and 166, each minus story should be interpreted as two rods placed side by side. The rod lengths are colored on the strips provided.

The conversion to numerals comes from relating the value of each rod to white rods. First, students translate the minus story into numbers. Then they write the complete subtraction sentence.

The master on page 167 is open-ended so that students or the teacher may pose additional examples. It should be noted that the first rod is longer than the second rod in these subtraction problems. Later on, the rods can be used for modeling negative numbers, but not at this stage of development.

Solutions

Writing Subtraction Sentences Worksheet 1 (p. 165)
1) dark green, red, purple   6 – 2   6 – 2 = 4
2) blue, green, dark green   9 – 3   9 – 3 = 6
3) orange, yellow, yellow   10 – 5   10 – 5 = 5
4) brown, purple, purple   8 – 4   8 – 4 = 4

Writing Subtraction Sentences Worksheet 2 (p. 166)
1) purple, white, green   4 – 1   4 – 1 = 3
2) dark green, purple, red   6 – 4   6 – 4 = 2
3) orange, red, brown   10 – 2   10 – 2 = 8
4) black, green, purple   7 – 3   7 – 3 = 4
5) blue, yellow, purple   9 – 5   9 – 5 = 4

Underlying Mathematics Related to the NCTM Standards:

Representation of lengths in terms of white rods
Association of numbers with rods
Recognition of equivalences of lengths
Use of minus sign
Use of subtraction sentences
Missing addends
Reasoning and proof
Communication and verbalization of ideas

Using a Number Line to Subtract

Materials

Cuisenaire Rods for each student
Pencil for each student
Using a Number Line to Subtract:
    Worksheet 1, page 168
    Worksheet 2, page 169
    Master, page 170

Settings

One student working individually
A small group, students working individually
A whole class, students working individually

Learning Experience

The number line model for subtraction involves placing the first rod with its left end at 0. The second rod length is subtracted off by placing it on top of the first rod so that their right ends match. The difference between the two rods can be read directly from the number line, as shown in the examples on the worksheets on pages 168 and 169.

It should be noted that the number lines for rods are gridded in centimeters, since the numerical interpretation is in terms of white rods.

The number line approach provides a visualization of the process of subtraction. Some students will find the use of number lines helpful. For those who do not, the worksheets on pages 168 and 169 should be omitted and considered as optional to the main development.

Using the master on page 170, students or the teacher may pose more subtraction problems to be done using number lines.

Solutions

Using a Number Line to Subtract Worksheet 1 (p. 168)
1) brown, dark green $8 - 6 = 2$
2) black, white $7 - 1 = 6$
3) dark green, purple $6 - 4 = 2$
4) blue, red $9 - 2 = 7$
5) brown, green $8 - 3 = 5$
6) orange, black $10 - 7 = 3$

Using a Number Line to Subtract Worksheet 2 (p. 169)
1) black, green $7 - 3 = 4$
2) yellow, red $5 - 2 = 3$
3) brown, white $8 - 1 = 7$
4) orange, purple $10 - 4 = 6$
5) brown, yellow $8 - 5 = 3$
6) blue, dark green $9 - 6 = 3$

Underlying Mathematics Related to the NCTM Standards:

Representation of lengths in terms of white rods
Association of numbers with rods
Meaning of subtraction
Use of minus sign
Connections between addition and subtraction
Reasoning and proof

Practicing Subtraction Sentences

Materials

Cuisenaire Rods for each student
Crayons matching the rod colors for each student
Pencil for each student
Practicing Subtraction Sentences:
    Worksheet 1, page 171
    Worksheet 2, page 172
    Master, page 173

Settings

One student working individually
A small group, students working individually
A whole class, students working individually

Learning Experience

The worksheets on pages 171 and 172 provide subtraction problems in the traditional arithmetic format. Students should be encouraged to interpret each problem with rods by coloring the rod picture to match the subtraction story. The gridded strips in centimeters reinforce the use of a white rod as representing the value 1. Once the difference is found and colored, students write the completed subtraction sentence.

It is important to go from numerals to rods and from rods to numerals to reinforce the subtraction facts being developed.

Repeated practice on worksheets like these is warranted. Hence, the master on page 173 is left open-ended so that further problems can be posed by students or by the teacher.

Solutions

Practicing Subtraction Sentences Worksheet 1 (p. 171)
1) yellow, white, purple   5 – 1 = 4
2) purple, red, red   4 – 2 = 2
3) black, purple, green   7 – 4 = 3
4) orange, green, black   10 – 3 = 7
5) blue, dark green, green   9 – 6 = 3

Practicing Subtraction Sentences Worksheet 2 (p. 172)
1) yellow, green, red   5 – 3 = 2
2) dark green, yellow, white   6 – 5 = 1
3) brown, purple, purple   8 – 4 = 4
4) orange, red, brown   10 – 2 = 8
5) blue, black, red   9 – 7 = 2
6) orange, dark green, purple   10 – 6 = 4

Underlying Mathematics Related to the NCTM Standards:

Representation of lengths in terms of white rods
Association of numbers with rods
Meaning of subtraction
Use of minus sign
Use of subtraction sentences
Connections between addition and subtraction
Reasoning and proof

Writing Addition and Subtraction Sentences

Materials
Cuisenaire Rods for each student
Pencil for each student
Writing Addition and Subtraction Sentences:
    Worksheet 1, page 174
    Worksheet 2, page 175
    Worksheet 3, page 176
Crayons matching the rod colors (optional)

Settings
One student working individually
A small group, students working individually
A whole class, students working individually

Learning Experience
All too often, the focus on arithmetic practice problems is on the numbers involved rather than the operations described. If the first problem on a page is addition, students often do all subsequent problems as addition. This is natural, since in teaching the operations we tend to treat each one separately. However, once the concepts have been established, students should have to deal with more than one process at a time.

The worksheets on pages 174–176 are engaging since students use the same three rods to do their own addition and subtraction sentences. The task should be kept light and enjoyable.

Solutions

Two addition sentences and two subtraction sentences should be given for each rod triple. All possible sentences are given here:

Writing Addition and Subtraction Sentences
Worksheet 1 (p. 174)

1) 1 + 4 = 5   5 – 1 = 4
   4 + 1 = 5   5 – 4 = 1
   5 = 1 + 4   4 = 5 – 1
   5 = 4 + 1   1 = 5 – 4

2) 3 + 5 = 8   8 – 3 = 5
   5 + 3 = 8   8 – 5 = 3
   8 = 3 + 5   5 = 8 – 3
   8 = 5 + 3   3 = 8 – 5

Writing Addition and Subtraction Sentences
Worksheet 2 (p. 175)

1) 2 + 8 = 10   10 – 2 = 8
   8 + 2 = 10   10 – 8 = 2
   10 = 2 + 8   8 = 10 – 2
   10 = 8 + 2   2 = 10 – 8

2) 5 + 3 = 8   8 – 5 = 3
   3 + 5 = 8   8 – 3 = 5
   8 = 5 + 3   3 = 8 – 5
   8 = 3 + 5   5 = 8 – 3

3) 3 + 2 = 5   5 – 3 = 2
   2 + 3 = 5   5 – 2 = 3
   5 = 3 + 2   2 = 5 – 3
   5 = 2 + 3   3 = 5 – 2

4) 4 + 6 = 10   10 – 4 = 6
   6 + 4 = 10   10 – 6 = 4
   10 = 4 + 6   6 = 10 – 4
   10 = 6 + 4   4 = 10 – 6

5) 4 + 5 = 9   9 – 5 = 4
   5 + 4 = 9   9 – 4 = 5
   9 = 4 + 5   4 = 9 – 5
   9 = 5 + 4   5 = 9 – 4

Writing Addition and Subtraction Sentences
Worksheet 3 (p. 176)

1) 3 + 6 = 9   9 – 3 = 6
   6 + 3 = 9   9 – 6 = 3
   9 = 3 + 6   6 = 9 – 3
   9 = 6 + 3   3 = 9 – 6

2) 8 + 2 = 10   10 – 8 = 2
   2 + 8 = 10   10 – 2 = 8
   10 = 8 + 2   2 = 10 – 8
   10 = 2 + 8   8 = 10 – 2

3) 5 + 3 = 8   8 – 5 = 3
   3 + 5 = 8   8 – 3 = 5
   8 = 5 + 3   3 = 8 – 5
   8 = 3 + 5   5 = 8 – 3

Underlying Mathematics Related to the NCTM Standards:
Association of numbers with rods
Use of the terms *rod triple* and *triple of rods*
Use of addition sentences
Use of subtraction sentences
Connections between addition and subtraction
Reasoning and proof

Extending the Staircase

Materials
Cuisenaire Rods for each student
Ruler for each student
Extra orange rods for each student

Settings
A small group led by the teacher
A whole class led by the teacher

Learning Experience
Ask each student to take one rod of each of the ten colors and to build a staircase using a ruler to establish a base line. Direct students to continue the staircase by using orange rods and one additional rod, so that each step "hops up" by the length of one white rod.

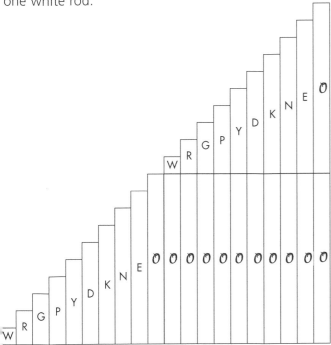

Interesting questions to ask students include the following:

- *Do you see a pattern?*

- *Close your eyes and "photograph" your staircase. What comes after "orange?" "orange plus red?" "orange plus blue?", etc.*

Ask students to write a plus story for each step after orange. (*O* + W, *O* + R, *O* + G, *O* + P, etc.)

Now ask students to cover each step with white rods. Have them write an addition story for each step beyond orange by describing lengths in terms of orange and white rods. (10 + 1, 10 + 2, 10 + 3, 10 + 4, etc.) Then ask: *What would the steps look like after two orange rods?* This experience helps to build readiness for two-digit numerals and an intuition for place value.

Underlying Mathematics Related to the NCTM Standards:
Representation of lengths in terms of white rods
Counting
Readiness for tens and ones
Place value (tens and ones)
Patterns
Communication and verbalization of ideas

Organizing Teen Numbers

Materials

Cuisenaire Rods for each student
Pencil for each student
Organizing Teen Numbers:
    Worksheet 1, page 177
    Worksheet 2, page 178

Settings

One student working individually
A small group, students working individually
A whole class, students working individually

Learning Experience

The worksheets on pages 177 and 178 develop the pictorial stage of the concrete level experienced on page 77.

The gridded strip at the bottom of the page serves as a pictorial representation of the white rods. Students should count the required number of white rods and match that length with an orange rod plus another rod. When they have completed the plus story with the correct letter codes, they complete the addition sentence with numerals. This activity builds readiness for place value and the process of regrouping into tens and ones.

Solutions

Organizing Teen Numbers Worksheet 1 (p. 177)
1) E   9
2) W   1
3) Y   5
4) R   2
5) K   7

Organizing Teen Numbers Worksheet 2 (p. 178)
1) N   8
2) O   10
3) Y   5
4) R   2
5) P   4
6) G   3
7) D   6

Underlying Mathematics Related to the NCTM Standards:

Representation of lengths in terms of white rods
Counting
Readiness for tens and ones
Place value (tens and ones)
Patterns
Reasoning and proof
Communication and verbalization of ideas

Playing Challenge Match for Sums

Materials
Cuisenaire Rods for each student

Settings
Two students working together
A small group, students working in pairs
A whole class, students working in pairs

Learning Experience

This is the third Challenge Match game in the development of addition and subtraction. This version extends the work on addition and helps students form equivalent lengths beyond orange.

Place 40–50 assorted rods in the center of the table for each pair of students. The first player chooses two rods and places them end to end in a train. The second player must find a one-car train or a two-car train that matches the first player's train. The second player keeps the rods involved in the match. Note that more than one match might be possible. For example, green plus purple could be matched with black (a one-car train) or it could be matched with red plus yellow (a two-car train) or white plus dark green (another two-car train).

Then the second player chooses two rods and challenges the first player to make a one-car train or a two-car train that matches. The first player keeps all the rods once the match has been made. The players reverse roles again. The pile of rods in the center of the table gets smaller each time. The object of the game is to make a challenge that cannot be matched with the remaining rods. The player to do this first wins the game and scores one point for each rod left in the center of the table. Students should play this game several times. They will enjoy alternating this game with the Challenge Match for Addends game on page 42.

Underlying Mathematics Related to the NCTM Standards:
Recognition of equivalences of lengths
Association of sums with addends
Association of various addends for a sum
Place value (tens and ones)
Visual thinking
Reasoning and proof
Communication and verbalization of ideas

Finding Sums Greater Than Orange

Materials

Cuisenaire Rods for each student
Crayons matching the rod colors for each student
Pencil for each student
Finding Sums Greater Than Orange:
  Worksheet 1, page 179
  Worksheet 2, page 180

Settings

One student working individually
A small group, students working individually
A whole class, students working individually

Learning Experience

The worksheets on pages 179 and 180 go in a progression. On the worksheet on page 179, students match each train picture with an orange rod plus another rod and then record the code for this other rod. The focus is on the amount beyond orange.

On the worksheet on page 180, students are given the codes for two rods whose sum is longer than orange. The train should be colored on the top strip of graph paper. Then the students match this train with an orange rod plus another rod. They may wish to color their orange-plus train as well. The orange-plus train is recorded with codes. The strips build readiness for the numerical stage that follows.

Solutions

Finding Sums Greater Than Orange Worksheet 1 (p. 179)
1) G + E = O + R
2) N + P = O + R
3) R + E = O + W
4) P + K = O + W
5) K + D = O + G
5) E + Y = O + P

Finding Sums Greater Than Orange Worksheet 2 (p. 180)
1) dark green, brown, orange, purple O + P
2) black, black, orange, purple O + P
3) blue, green, orange, red O + R
4) brown, black, orange, yellow O + Y

Underlying Mathematics Related to the NCTM Standards:

Representation of lengths in terms of white rods
Recognition of equivalences of lengths
Association of sums with addends
Place value (tens and ones)
Reasoning and proof
Communication and verbalization of ideas

Writing Addition Sentences for Sums Greater Than Orange

Materials
Cuisenaire Rods for each student
Crayons matching the rod colors for each student
Pencil for each student
Writing Addition Sentences for Sums
  Greater Than Orange:
    Worksheet 1, page 181
    Worksheet 2, page 182
    Worksheet 3, page 183

Settings
One student working individually
A small group, students working individually
A whole class, students working individually

Learning Experience

The series of worksheets on pages 181–183 helps students make the transition from rods to numbers for sums beyond ten.

In coloring the given train on the gridded strips on worksheet pages 181 and 182, students are intuitively associating the rod lengths with an equivalent train of white rods. Each train is then matched with an orange plus train. The resulting length in terms of white rods should be expressed first as 10 + ___ and then written as a two-digit numeral.

The worksheet on page 183 encourages students to use the rods only when needed. Some students will be able to use logical thinking from the work with the missing addends. For example, 8 + 3 can be thought of as starting with 8, needing 2 more to make 10, and having 1 left from the 3. Hence, 8 + 3 = 10 + 1, or 11. The last four addition problems are given in vertical form rather than horizontal form. The vertical form emphasizes the concept of place value (tens and ones).

Solutions

Writing Addition Sentences for Sums Greater
Than Orange Worksheet 1 (p. 181)
1) 2 + 9 = 10 + 1 = 11
2) 8 + 6 = 10 + 4 = 14
3) 7 + 7 = 10 + 4 = 14
4) 5 + 6 = 10 + 1 = 11
5) 3 + 9 = 10 + 2 = 12

Writing Addition Sentences for Sums Greater
Than Orange Worksheet 2 (p. 182)
1) 4 + 9 = 10 + 3 = 13
2) 5 + 7 = 10 + 2 = 12
3) 9 + 8 = 10 + 7 = 17
4) 6 + 9 = 10 + 5 = 15

Writing Addition Sentences for Sums Greater
Than Orange Worksheet 3 (p. 183)

1) 12		**7)** 16	
2) 12		**8)** 16	
3) 15		**9)** 15	
4) 14		**10)** 18	
5) 11		**11)** 12	
6) 14		**12)** 18	

Underlying Mathematics Related to the NCTM Standards:
Representation of lengths in terms of white rods
Association of sums with addends
Use of addition sentences
Place value (tens and ones)
Reasoning and proof
Communication and verbalization of ideas

Using a Number Line for Sums Greater Than 10

Materials

Cuisenaire Rods for each student
Pencil for each student
Using a Number Line for Sums Greater Than 10:
    Worksheet 1, page 184
    Worksheet 2, page 185
    Master, page 186

Settings

One student working individually
A small group, students working individually
A whole class, students working individually

Learning Experience

The worksheets on pages 184 and 185 are extensions of the number line model introduced on page 59. Here, the emphasis is on sums between 10 and 20. The length of a white rod serves as the unit, since the number line is gridded in centimeters.

The rod representing the first addend is placed with its left end at 0. The rod for the second addend is placed so that the rods are end to end in a train. The total length can be read directly from where the right end of the second addend touches the number line.

The master on page 186 is open-ended for further practice as needed. This same master also can be used for subtraction through 20, following the work on page 85 and the model for number line subtraction on page 74.

Solutions

Using a Number Line for Sums Greater Than 10 Worksheet 1 (p. 184)
1) yellow, brown   5 + 8 = 13
2) purple, black   4 + 7 = 11
3) blue, purple   9 + 4 = 13

Using a Number Line for Sums Greater Than 10 Worksheet 2 (p. 185)
1) dark green, black   6 + 7 = 13
2) blue, yellow   9 + 5 = 14
3) brown, purple   8 + 4 = 12
4) dark green, dark green   6 + 6 = 12
5) brown, blue   8 + 9 = 17

Underlying Mathematics Related to the NCTM Standards:
Recognition of equivalences of lengths
Representation of lengths in terms of white rods
Association of sums with addends
Use of addition sentences
Counting
Place value (tens and ones)
Reasoning and proof

Making an Addition Table for Sums Through 20

Materials

Cuisenaire Rods for each student
Pencil for each student
Making an Addition Table for Sums Through 20
    Worksheet, page 187

Settings

One student working individually
A small group, students working individually
A whole class, students working individually

Learning Experience

The worksheet on page 187 extends the addition table developed on page 60 to include sums through 20. Once this worksheet is completed, students should keep it for reference while doing addition and subtraction problems.

Also, it is helpful to have a large poster of this addition table to display on a bulletin board. Students will enjoy helping to make it. Having the correct facts visible in the classroom helps students learn them in much the same way that the posting of the upper-case and lower-case letters helps students with writing and printing.

Students should discuss the patterns in the table. This will help them use the commutative property of addition, relate the facts to one another, and visualize all the combinations that result in the same sum. They will enjoy studying the constant sums that lie on the diagonals going from the upper right to the lower left. They also will enjoy observing when a sum is even and when a sum is odd. If both addends are odd or both addends are even, the sum is even. Only when one addend is odd and the other is even will the sum be odd.

Solutions

Making an Addition Table for Sums Through 20 Worksheet (p. 187)

+	1	2	3	4	5	6	7	8	9	10
1	2	3	4	5	6	7	8	9	10	11
2	3	4	5	6	7	8	9	10	11	12
3	4	5	6	7	8	9	10	11	12	13
4	5	6	7	8	9	10	11	12	13	14
5	6	7	8	9	10	11	12	13	14	15
6	7	8	9	10	11	12	13	14	15	16
7	8	9	10	11	12	13	14	15	16	17
8	9	10	11	12	13	14	15	16	17	18
9	10	11	12	13	14	15	16	17	18	19
10	11	12	13	14	15	16	17	18	19	20

Underlying Mathematics Related to the NCTM Standards:

Representation of lengths in terms of white rods
Association of sums with addends
Meaning of addition
Commutative property of addition
Use of table with rows and columns
Patterns
Even and odd numbers
Communication and verbalization of ideas

Checking Addition Facts Through 20

Materials
Cuisenaire Rods for each student
Pencil for each student
Checking Addition Facts Through 20
    Worksheet, page 188
1-cm Graph Paper Master, page 99

Settings
One student working individually
A small group, students working individually
A whole class, students working individually

Learning Experience
The worksheet on page 188 is the final one in the series on addition of two numbers whose sum is between 10 and 20. As a culminating exercise, students may work entirely on the abstract level or on the pictorial level by counting squares on centimeter graph paper. If students need a more concrete level, they can use rods on the number line provided at the bottom of the worksheet or build trains and match them with orange plus trains.

The important aspects are for students to be able to relate numbers to rod lengths, to understand the concept of addition, and to think in terms of tens and ones. These aspects occur regardless of whether students are working on a concrete, pictorial, or abstract level.

Solutions
Checking Addition Facts Through 20 Worksheet (p. 188)

1) 13		**9)** 14	
2) 14		**10)** 17	
3) 16		**11)** 11	
4) 13		**12)** 12	
5) 17		**13)** 11	
6) 14		**14)** 15	
7) 11		**15)** 18	
8) 15		**16)** 16	

Underlying Mathematics Related to the NCTM Standards:
Representation of lengths in terms of white rods
Association of sums with addends
Use of addition sentences
Counting
Place value (tens and ones)
Reasoning and proof
Communication and verbalization of ideas

Subtracting from Teen Numbers

Materials
Cuisenaire Rods for each student

Settings
A small group led by the teacher
A whole class led by the teacher

Learning Experience

Choose an orange plus train and another rod. Ask students to subtract the single rod from the orange plus train. For example:

"orange plus green" minus "dark green"

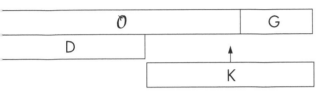

Using the white rods as ones, write the following subtraction sentence: 13 – 6 = 7

Provide students with several more subtraction stories like this one. The rod model shows clearly the inverse relationship between addition and subtraction. In solving the subtraction problem, the students actually build the train for the corresponding addition problem.

The rod model also helps to build readiness for regrouping in subtraction and for viewing place value (tens and ones).

Underlying Mathematics Related to the NCTM Standards:
Recognition of equivalences of lengths
Representation of lengths in terms of white rods
Use of subtraction sentences
Connections between addition and subtraction
Readiness for regrouping in subtraction
Reasoning and proof
Communication and verbalization of ideas

Practicing Subtraction Sentences with Teen Numbers

Materials

Cuisenaire Rods for each student
Crayons matching the rod colors
Pencil for each student
Practicing Subtraction Sentences with Teen Numbers:
    Worksheet 1, page 189
    Worksheet 2, page 190
    Master, page 191

Settings

One student working individually
A small group, students working individually
A whole class, students working individually

Learning Experience

Addition facts were developed for sums through 20 in the learning experience on page 83. Students should now be able to work out the inverse operation for any of these facts. This may involve subtracting from two-digit numbers.

On the worksheets on pages 189 and 190, each subtraction story can be translated into an orange plus train minus another rod. Students should color the pictures for their stories on the graph paper strips. They should find and color the rod for the difference and write the complete subtraction sentence. These strips really give a visual sense of when regrouping in subtraction is necessary.

The master on page 191 is open-ended to provide practice as necessary prior to the more abstract problem set on the worksheet on page 192.

Solutions

Practicing Subtraction Sentences with Teen Numbers Worksheet 1 (p. 189)
1) orange plus brown, blue, blue $18 - 9 = 9$
2) orange plus green, dark green, black $13 - 6 = 7$
3) orange plus orange, black, orange plus green $20 - 7 = 13$
4) orange plus purple, brown, dark green $14 - 8 = 6$

Practicing Subtraction Sentences Worksheet 2 (p. 190)
1) orange plus white, yellow, dark green $11 - 5 = 6$
2) orange plus black, black, orange $17 - 7 = 10$
3) orange plus purple, blue, yellow $14 - 9 = 5$
4) orange plus brown, red, orange plus dark green $18 - 2 = 16$
5) orange plus yellow, dark green, blue $15 - 6 = 9$

Underlying Mathematics Related to the NCTM Standards:

Recognition of equivalences of lengths
Representation of lengths in terms of white rods
Use of subtraction sentences
Readiness for regrouping in subtraction
Connections between addition and subtraction
Reasoning and proof
Communication and verbalization of ideas

Checking Subtraction Facts

Materials

Cuisenaire Rods for each student
Pencil for each student
Checking Subtraction Facts Worksheet, page 192

Settings

One student working individually
A small group, students working individually
A whole class, students working individually

Learning Experience

Students are asked to complete subtraction problems without the use of rods. The worksheet on page 192 is the final one in the series on subtraction problems through 20.

As a culminating exercise, some students may be able to work entirely at the abstract level. Others may need to use the rods on some or all of the problems.

The number line at the bottom of the worksheet allows students to either check or do the problems using rods. The entire development in this book encourages students to be self-checking, for the rod model lends itself nicely to fostering independence in thinking.

Solutions

Checking Subtraction Facts Worksheet (p. 192)

1) 5		**9)** 6	
2) 7		**10)** 10	
3) 6		**11)** 9	
4) 8		**12)** 4	
5) 8		**13)** 8	
6) 7		**14)** 5	
7) 7		**15)** 8	
8) 9		**16)** 9	

Underlying Mathematics Related to the NCTM Standards:

Representation of lengths in terms of white rods
Use of subtraction sentences
Readiness for regrouping in subtraction
Connections between addition and subtraction
Reasoning and proof
Communication and verbalization of ideas

Mastering Addition and Subtraction Through 20

Materials

Cuisenaire Rods for each student
Crayons matching the rod colors
Pencil for each student
Mastering Addition and Subtraction Through 20:
    Worksheet 1, page 193
    Worksheet 2, page 194

Settings

One student working individually
A small group, students working individually
A whole class, students working individually

Learning Experience

On the worksheets on pages 193 and 194, a mixture of addition and subtraction problems is given at the abstract level.

The worksheet on page 193 gives the problems in the horizontal format using the equal sign. The worksheet on page 194 uses a vertical format and puts the emphasis on place value (tens and ones).

Students may use rods on the number line at the bottom of the page to check their answers and to find any answers that they do not readily know by heart.

Solutions

Mastering Addition and Subtraction Through 20 Worksheet 1 (p. 193)
1) 14
2) 2
3) 7
4) 14
5) 6
6) 14
7) 15
8) 11
9) 3
10) 10
11) 7
12) 17
13) 5
14) 7

Mastering Addition and Subtraction Through 20 Worksheet 2 (p. 194)
1) 9
2) 3
3) 12
4) 2
5) 14
6) 5
7) 7
8) 13
9) 8
10) 16
11) 7
12) 15

Underlying Mathematics Related to the NCTM Standards:

Representation of lengths in terms of white rods
Use of addition sentences
Use of subtraction sentences
Connections between addition and subtraction
Reasoning and proof
Communication and verbalization of ideas

Hitting the Target Number Game

Materials
Cuisenaire Rods for each student
30 index cards for each pair of students

Settings
Two students working together
A small group, students working in pairs
A whole class, students working in pairs

Learning Experience
This game may be played with rods and then with numbers.

Rod Version
Make a deck of 30 cards consisting of 3 cards for each of the 10 rod codes. Place the deck face down between partners. The partners agree on a target for the round; for example, two orange rods. On each turn, the player takes the top card from the deck and either adds or subtracts that rod length from the value thus far in the game. As the game progresses, a player may go beyond the target value, and then the other player will bring the value below the target by subtracting. The first player to hit the target exactly wins the game. The rods should be used to show each stage of the game.

Sample game:

Player 1:	green	"Add"	Value: 3
Player 2:	brown	"Add"	Value: 11
Player 1:	orange	"Add"	Value: 21
Player 2:	red	"Subtract"	Value: 19
Player 1:	white	"Add"	Value: 20 Winner!

Number Version
Make a deck of 30 cards consisting of 3 cards for each of the numerals 0–9. Place the deck face down between the partners. The partners agree on a target number for the round; for example, 20. On each turn, the player takes the top card from the deck and chooses to add to or subtract from the value thus far in the game. The goal is to hit the target number exactly.

Sample game:

Player 1:	5	"Add"	Value: 5
Player 2:	9	"Add"	Value: 14
Player 1:	8	"Add"	Value: 22
Player 2:	2	"Subtract"	Value: 20 Winner!

Larger target numbers should be selected as students gain experience with the game.

Underlying Mathematics Related to the NCTM Standards:
Association of rods with codes
Regrouping in addition
Readiness for regrouping in subtraction
Connections between addition and subtraction
Communication and verbalization of ideas

Finding Sums with More Than Two Addends

Materials

Cuisenaire Rods for each student
Crayons matching the rod colors (optional)
Pencil for each student
Finding Sums with More Than Two Addends:
    Worksheet 1, page 195
    Worksheet 2, page 196

Settings

One student working individually
A small group, students working individually
A whole class, students working individually

Learning Experience

The worksheets on pages 195 and 196 present addition problems with three addends. The problems have been carefully chosen to encourage students to look for combinations that make 10.

It is very helpful for students to see 8 + 1 + 9 as 8 + 10, or 18 or 1 + 3 + 9 as 10 + 3, or 13. From all of their rearranging of the cars in rod trains, students should realize addition can be done in any order. Encouraging students to see that there is more than one way to get a correct answer helps them become self-checking, accurate, and confident in their mathematical abilities.

The worksheet on page 195 encourages students to use rods on the gridded strips to obtain the complete addition sentence. The worksheet on page 196 encourages students to find as many sums as possible without the use of the rods and then to use the rods to check their answers or to solve particularly difficult problems. The last six problems are given in vertical format.

Solutions

Finding Sums with More Than Two Addends Worksheet 1 (p. 195)
1) purple, white, yellow, orange   10
2) dark green, brown, red, orange plus dark green   16
3) purple, purple, dark green, orange plus purple   14
4) black, green, yellow, orange plus yellow   15
5) brown, blue, white, orange plus brown   18

Finding Sums with More Than Two Addends Worksheet 2 (p. 196)
1) red, green, purple, blue   9
2) black, brown, yellow, orange plus orange   20
3) dark green, white, red, blue   9
4) dark green, yellow, purple, orange plus yellow   15
5) red, black, yellow, orange plus purple   14
6) green, brown, purple, orange plus yellow   15
7) yellow, yellow, green, orange plus green   13
8) brown, red, orange, orange plus orange   20
9) blue, green, white, orange plus green   13
10) black, red, green, orange plus red   12
11) dark green, yellow, black, orange plus brown   18
12) yellow, black, yellow, orange plus black   17
13) brown, purple, red, orange plus purple   14
14) white, brown, blue, orange plus brown   18

Underlying Mathematics Related to the NCTM Standards:

Representation of lengths in terms of white rods
Regrouping in addition
Association of sums with addends
Use of addition sentences
Sums with more than two addends
Reasoning and proof
Communication and verbalization of ideas

Finding the Value of Rod Code Words

Materials
Cuisenaire Rods for each student
Pencil for each student
Finding the Value of Rod Code Words:
    Worksheet 1, page 197
    Worksheet 2, page 198
    Master, page 199

Settings
One student working individually
A small group, students working individually
A small group, students working in pairs

Learning Experience

The worksheets on pages 197 and 198 are similar to those on pages 109 and 110, but here students are not only asked to find the rod codes for the given number of white rods, they are also asked to find the total value of each word in terms of white rods. Some students enjoy attaching money values to the rod code words, with W costing 1 cent, R costing 2 cents, G costing 3 cents, etc.

The master on page 199 can be used in two ways:
1) Teachers can use the suggested list of rod words or the ones given on page 30 and give the number of white rods needed for each letter. The students find the rod word and its total value in terms of white rods.
2) Teachers can use the words listed below and let students give the number of white rods needed for each letter and then find the total value.

Some words that might be used for further work:
Three-letter words: dew, pep, key, nod, woe, wok, own, owe, row, wed, dye, ore, pod, egg, now
Four-letter words: keen, neon, open, rode, gone, drew, word, gong, wore, were, deed, done, none, weed, deer, gene, noon, nook, reed, woke, redo, wood, word, work
Five-letter words: prong, error, dodge, erode, known, green, grope, poppy, prone, peppy, perky, owner, wrong, needy, wordy, poker
Six-letter words: powder, render, depend, groggy, Oregon, deepen, greedy, pepper, dredge, energy, wonder, wooden, worker, proton, gender, proper
Seven-letter words: prodded, weekend, reorder, dropped
Eight-letter words: greenery, ponderer

Students should be encouraged to think up other words. If students think of words that use letters other than the rod codes, they learn from noting what letters are not correct rod codes.

Solutions

Finding the Value of Rod Code Words Worksheet 1 (p. 197)
1) DEN   6 + 9 + 8 = 23
2) PROD   4 + 2 + 10 + 6 = 22
3) KNEE   7 + 8 + 9 + 9 = 33
4) EDGE   9 + 6 + 3 + 9 = 27
5) NOW   8 + 10 + 1 = 19
6) ORDER   10 + 2 + 6 + 9 + 2 = 29

Finding the Value of Rod Code Words Worksheet 2 (p. 198)
1) PEN   4 + 9 + 8 = 21
2) DROP   6 + 2 + 10 + 4 = 22
3) DOOR   6 + 10 + 10 + 2 = 28
4) KNEW   7 + 8 + 9 + 1 = 25
5) NONE   8 + 10 + 8 + 9 = 35
6) RYE   2 + 5 + 9 = 16
7) KNOWN   7 + 8 + 10 + 1 + 8 = 34

Underlying Mathematics Related to the NCTM Standards:

Representation of lengths in terms of white rods
Association of rods with codes
Association of codes with rods
Association of codes with words
Counting
Sums with more than two addends

Regrouping in addition
Money values
Connections to real-life experiences
Problem solving
Communication and verbalization of ideas

Finding the Value of Rod Designs

Materials
Cuisenaire Rods for each student
Pencil for each student
Finding the Value of Rod Designs:
    Worksheet 1, page 200
    Worksheet 2, page 201

Settings
One student working individually
A small group, students working individually
A small group, students working in pairs

Learning Experience

On the worksheets on pages 200 and 201, the study of addition with more than two addends is extended to a format in which the problems can be done in many ways.

Students cover each design with rods, and then they find the total value of all of these rods in terms of white rods. Some students may wish to make a long train and match it with a train of orange rods plus another rod. Others may want to match their rods with white rods. Many students will be able to write the correct addition sentence immediately and do the adding in their heads.

Each design should be done in several different ways. This exercise builds readiness for multiplication as repeated addition, since more than one rod of the same color is often used within a single design.

Some students will enjoy attaching money values to the rods used in making a design, with a white rod costing 1 cent, a red rod costing 2 cents, a green rod costing 3 cents, etc. For more designs, repeat the building and coloring experience on pages 16–18.

Solutions

The addition sentences will depend on how each design is covered.
Finding the Value of Rod Designs Worksheet 1 (p. 200)
1) Three green rods and two black rods can be placed horizontally:
$3 + 3 + 3 + 7 + 7 = 23$ (or $3 \times 3 + 2 \times 7 = 23$)
Four red rods and three yellow rods can be placed vertically:
$2 + 2 + 5 + 5 + 5 + 2 + 2 = 23$ (or $4 \times 2 + 3 \times 5 = 23$)

Finding the Value of Rod Designs Worksheet 2 (p. 201)
1) White, red, green, purple, and yellow can be placed horizontally:
$1 + 2 + 3 + 4 + 5 = 15$
Red and white can be placed horizontally as follows: white, red, white, red, red, red, white, red, red:
$1 + 1 + 1 + 2 + 2 + 2 + 2 + 2 + 2 = 15$ (or $3 \times 1 + 6 \times 2 = 15$)
2) White, red, green, purple, yellow, dark green can be placed horizontally or vertically:
$1 + 2 + 3 + 4 + 5 + 6 = 21$

2) Two purple rods and three dark green rods can be placed horizontally:
$4 + 4 + 6 + 6 + 6 = 26$ (or $2 \times 4 + 3 \times 6 = 26$)
Four red rods and six green rods can be placed vertically:
$2 + 2 + 2 + 2 + 3 + 3 + 3 + 3 + 3 + 3 = 26$ (or $4 \times 2 + 6 \times 3 = 26$)

3) Five orange rods can be placed horizontally:
$10 + 10 + 10 + 10 + 10 = 50$ (or $5 \times 10 = 50$)
Ten yellow rods can be vertically:
$5 + 5 + 5 + 5 + 5 + 5 + 5 + 5 + 5 + 5 = 50$ (or $10 \times 5 = 50$)
4) Three red rods, one purple rod, and one orange rod can be placed horizontally and vertically:
$2 + 2 + 2 + 4 + 10 + 10 = 30$ (or $3 \times 2 + 4 + 2 \times 10 = 30$)
Four purple rods, two green rods, and four red rods can be placed vertically:
$4 + 4 + 4 + 4 + 3 + 3 + 2 + 2 + 2 + 2 = 30$
(or $4 \times 4 + 2 \times 3 + 4 \times 2 = 30$)

Underlying Mathematics Related to the NCTM Standards:

NCTM

Representation of lengths in terms of white rods
Association of sums with addends
Use of addition sentences
Sums with more than two addends
Regrouping in addition
Money values

Multiplication as repeated addition
Connections between arithmetic and geometry
Symmetry
Visual thinking
Reasoning and proof
Communication and verbalization of ideas

Playing the Skip Counting by Tens Game

Materials
White and orange rods for each group
One die or two dice for each group

Settings
A small group working together
A whole class working in small groups

Learning Experience

Choose one student in each group to be a Banker. The Banker does not play the game, but is in charge of the white and orange rods. The student on the Banker's left starts the game. The player tosses the die and asks the Banker for that number of white rods.

Whenever a player is able to trade 10 white rods for 1 orange rod, this trade is done before the player passes the die on to the next player. At the end of each turn, the player tells the value accumulated thus far. For example, if the player had 3 orange rods and 4 white rods, the value would be expressed as 34. The value can be found by counting by tens (10, 20, 30) and then by ones (1, 2, 3, 4) to give 34.

The first player to accumulate four orange rods exactly (a score of 40) wins the game. A player may have to wait for the correct toss to end with exactly four orange rods. This delay allows other players to catch up, which makes the game more fun. The probability of getting a particular value (1, 2, 3, 4, 5, or 6) on a fair die is one-sixth.

The winner becomes the Banker for the next game. Students enjoy playing this game many times and often choose to play during free-choice times, outside of mathematics class. When the students feel ready, they can toss two dice and get that many white rods on a turn. The goal can be extended to 10 orange rods, so that the students have to skip count by tens to 100 (10, 20, 30, 40, etc.). Extra orange rods will need to be borrowed from other sets of rods. Those students can be playing the similar games on page 94, which use only red and yellow rods.

Students often like to think of the rods in terms of money, where a white rod is worth a penny (one cent) and an orange rod is worth a dime (10 cents). Thinking in terms of money seems like a different game to the students, and a very worthwhile one.

Underlying Mathematics Related to the NCTM Standards:
Representation of lengths in terms of white rods
Association of sums with addends
Place value (tens and ones)
Skip counting by tens
Multiplication as repeated addition
Money values
Patterns
Communication and verbalization of ideas

Playing the Skip Counting by Twos and by Fives Games

Materials
Red rods or yellow rods for each group
One die for each group

Settings
A small group working together
A whole class working in small groups

Learning Experience

Skip Counting by Twos Game
Choose one student in each group to be a Banker. The Banker does not play the game, but is in charge of the red rods. Extra red rods should be borrowed from the various sets of rods in the classroom while those students are playing the game for tens, which uses only white and orange rods (described on page 93) or the game for fives, which uses only yellow rods (described below).

The student on the Banker's left starts the game. The player tosses the die and asks the Banker for that many red rods and counts by twos. For example, if a 3 comes up on the die, on the first turn, the player gets 3 red rods and says aloud 2, 4, 6. Then, if this same player tosses a 4 on the second turn, the player gets 4 red rods and says aloud his total value of 14, by skip counting by twos: 2, 4, 6, 8, 10, 12, 14. The players take turns. The first player to have the exact value of 40 (20 red rods) wins the game. A player may have to wait for the correct toss to end with exactly 20 red rods. This delay allows other players to catch up, which adds to the fun and challenge. The winner becomes the Banker for the next game.

Skip Counting by Fives Game
Again, choose one student in each group to be a Banker. Extra yellow rods should be borrowed from the various sets of rods in the classroom while those students are playing the game for tens, which uses only white and orange rods (described on page 93) or the game for twos. This time, the value of the toss indicates the number of yellow rods the player gets from the Banker. The goal is to count by fives each time and to get to the exact value of 100 (20 yellow rods). Often, students think of the yellow rods as nickels (5 cents), with the goal of reaching the value of 100 cents or one dollar.

Mixing the Games
If a whole class is playing the three different games in small groups, the winners can move to a new group each time going clockwise around the room. The games may not end exactly at the same time, so the students in each group can use any extra time to say in unison the skip counting sequences for their number (2, 5, or 10) forwards and backwards.

Underlying Mathematics Related to the NCTM Standards:

Representation of lengths in terms of white rods	Multiplication as repeated addition
Association of sums with addends	Money values
Skip counting by twos	Patterns
Skip counting by fives	Communication and verbalization of ideas

Solving Rod Word Problems Using Addition and Subtraction

Materials

Solving Rod Word Problems:
    Worksheet 1, page 202
    Worksheet 2, page 203
    Worksheet 3, page 204

Settings

One student working individually
A small group, students working individually
A whole class, students working in individually

Learning Experience

The worksheets on pages 202 and 203 give a sampling of word problem situations that involve puzzles with rods and numbers. In either case, the entire worksheet of problems need not be done at one time. Rather, one or two problems could be given at a time and, when solved, the students could help to make similar problems to be shared and solved. Some of the problems have many possible answers. As a team, some students might be able to find most or all of the possible answers, but that is not a necessary goal for all students. It is important that students learn to make up problems, deal with problems that have more than one correct answer, and deal with problems that cannot be instantly solved.

The worksheet on page 204 gives students practice with word meanings as well as addition. Simple definitions of all the rod words suggested in the previous Rod Code learning experiences (pages 30 and 91) can be presented as additional puzzles for students to solve. Vocabulary building with the rods is as important as the addition practice. Solutions to all three worksheets can be found on the next page.

Underlying Mathematics Related to the NCTM Standards:

Representation of lengths in terms of white rods
Association of codes with rods
Use of addition sentences
Use of subtraction sentences
Even and odd numbers

Problem solving
Patterns
Connections to real-life experiences
Communication and verbalization of ideas

Solutions to Rod Word Problems

Solving Rod Word Problems Worksheet 1 (p. 202)
1) 1 + 2 + 3 + 4 + 5 + 6 + 7 + 8 + 9 + 10 = 55
2) 2 + 4 + 6 + 8 + 10 = 30
3) 1 + 3 + 5 + 7 + 9 = 25
4) 30 + 25 = 55; The five even rods plus the five odd rods make up the set of 10 rods.
5) 2 + 2 + 2 + 2 + 2 + 3 + 3 + 3 + 4 = 10 + 9 + 4 = 23
6) 1 + 2 + 3 + 7 = 13; 17 − 13 = 4
Hence, the fifth rod is purple.
7) 2 + 3 + 4 + 6 + 8 = 23; 30 − 23 = 7
Hence, the sixth rod is black.

Solving Rod Word Problems Worksheet 2 (p. 203)
1) The two colors are blue and dark green, since the numbers are 9 and 6.
2) The color is yellow, since 3 × 5 = 15.
3) The two colors are blue and purple, since the two numbers are 9 and 4.
4) The color is red, since 6 × 2 = 12.
5) Since 2 + 8 + 10 = 20, the rods could be red, brown, and orange or since 4 + 6 + 10 = 20, the rods could be purple, dark green and orange.
6) There are several possible answers. A student may give any four of these.
Since 1 + 4 + 10 = 15, the rods could be white, purple, and orange.
Since 1 + 5 + 9 = 15, the rods could be white, yellow, and blue.
Since 1 + 6 + 8 = 15, the rods could be white, dark green, and brown.
Since 2 + 3 + 10 = 15, the rods could be red, green, and orange.
Since 2 + 4 + 9 = 15, the rods could be red, purple, and blue.
Since 2 + 5 + 8 = 15, the rods could be red, yellow, and brown.
Since 2 + 6 + 7 = 15, the rods could be red, dark green, and black.
Since 3 + 4 + 8 = 15, the rods could be green, purple, and brown.
Since 3 + 5 + 7 = 15, the rods could be green, yellow, and black.
Since 4 + 5 + 6 = 15, the rods could be purple, yellow, and dark green.
7) There are several possible answers. A student may give any four of these.
Since 1 + 2 + 7 + 8 = 18, the rods could be white, red, black, and brown.
Since 1 + 2 + 6 + 9 = 18, the rods could be white, red, dark green, and blue.
Since 1 + 2 + 5 + 10 = 18, the rods could be white, red, yellow, and orange.
Since 1 + 3 + 6 + 8 = 18, the rods could be white, green, dark green, and brown.
Since 1 + 3 + 5 + 9 = 18, the rods could be white, green, yellow, and blue.
Since 1 + 3 + 4 + 10 = 18, the rods could be white, green, purple, and orange.
Since 1 + 4 + 5 + 8 = 18, the rods could be white, purple, yellow, and brown.
Since 1 + 4 + 6 + 7 = 18, the rods could be white, purple, dark green, and black.
Since 2 + 3 + 6 + 7 = 18, the rods could be red, green, dark green, and black.
Since 2 + 3 + 5 + 8 = 18, the rods could be red, green, yellow, and brown.
Since 2 + 3 + 4 + 9 = 18, the rods could be red, green, purple, and blue.
Since 2 + 4 + 5 + 7 = 18, the rods could be red, purple, yellow, and black.
Since 3 + 4 + 5 + 6 = 18, the rods could be green, purple, yellow, and dark green.

Solving Rod Word Problems Worksheet 3 (p. 204)

1) GREEN	3 + 2 + 9 + 9 + 8 = 31	
2) EYE	9 + 5 + 9 = 23	
3) KNEE	7 + 8 + 9 + 9 = 33	
4) PEN	4 + 9 + 8 = 21	
5) RODEO	2 + 10 + 6 + 9 + 10 = 37	
6) RED	2 + 9 + 6 = 17	
7) POND	4 + 10 + 8 + 6 = 28	
8) WEEK	1 + 9 + 9 + 7 = 26	
9) NEW YORK	8 + 9 + 1 + 5 + 10 + 2 + 7 = 42	
10) EGG	9 + 3 + 3 = 15	
11) DRY	6 + 2 + 5 = 13	
12) GOWN	3 + 10 + 1 + 8 = 22	

Name _____ Date _____

1. Put rods on each picture so that they match.
2. Remove each rod.
3. Color the pictures with the correct rod colors.

1.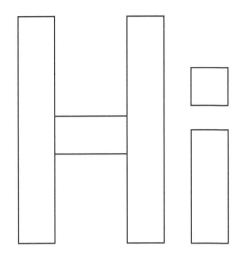

2.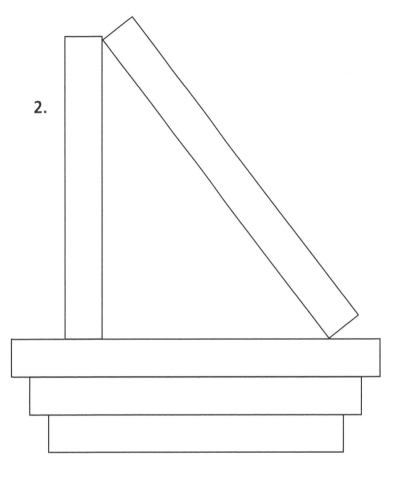

3.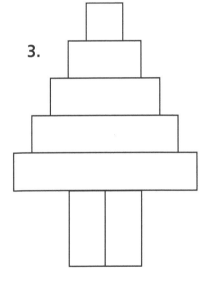

4.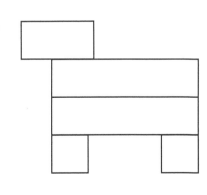

5.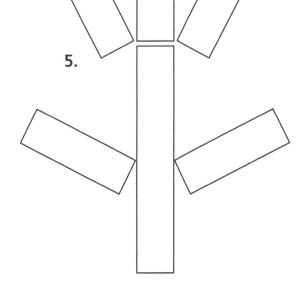

Making Rod Pictures
Worksheet 1

Name _____ Date _____

1. Put rods on each picture so that they match.
2. Remove each rod.
3. Color the pictures with the correct rod colors.

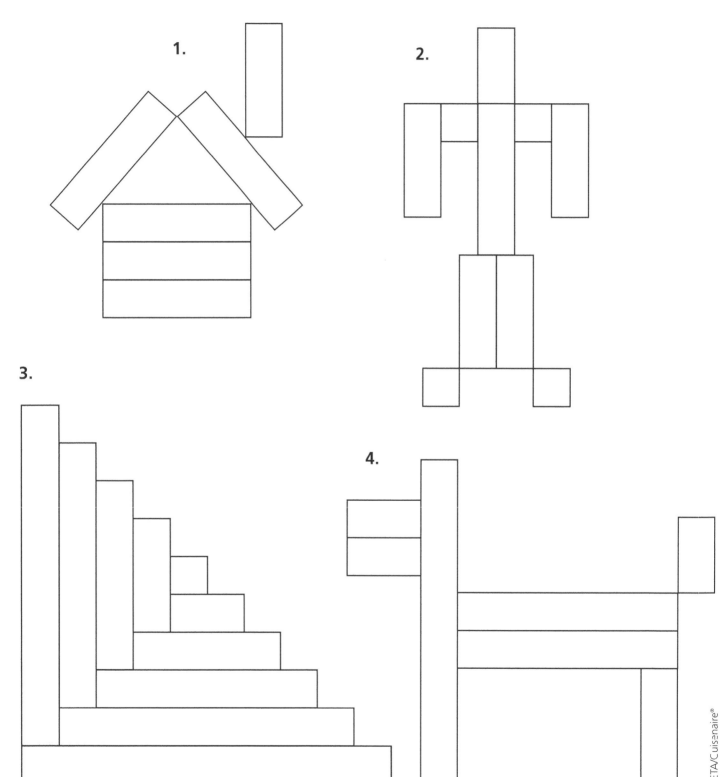

Addition & Subtraction with Cuisenaire® Rods

Making Rod Pictures
Worksheet 2

© ETA/Cuisenaire®

Name _____ Date _____

Addition & Subtraction with Cuisenaire® Rods

Name _____ Date _____

1. Write the correct code on each rod.
2. Color the pictures with the correct rod colors.

W	for	White	D	for	Dark green
R	for	Red	K	for	blacK
G	for	Green	N	for	browN
P	for	Purple	E	for	bluE
Y	for	Yellow	O	for	Orange

1.

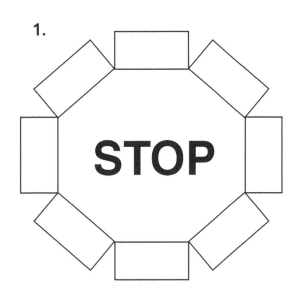

2.

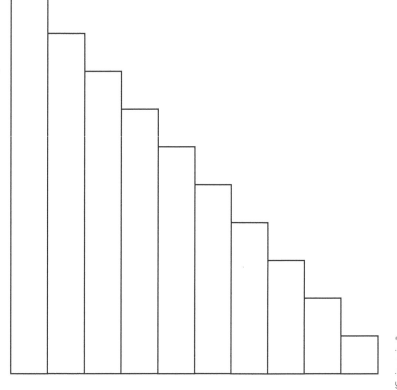

3.

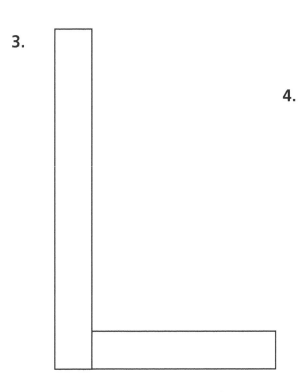

4.

Addition & Subtraction with Cuisenaire® Rods

Practicing Rod Codes
Worksheet 1

© ETA/Cuisenaire®

Name _____ Date _____

1. Write the correct code on each rod.
2. Color the pictures with the correct rod colors.

W	for	White	D	for	Dark green
R	for	Red	K	for	blacK
G	for	Green	N	for	browN
P	for	Purple	E	for	bluE
Y	for	Yellow	O	for	Orange

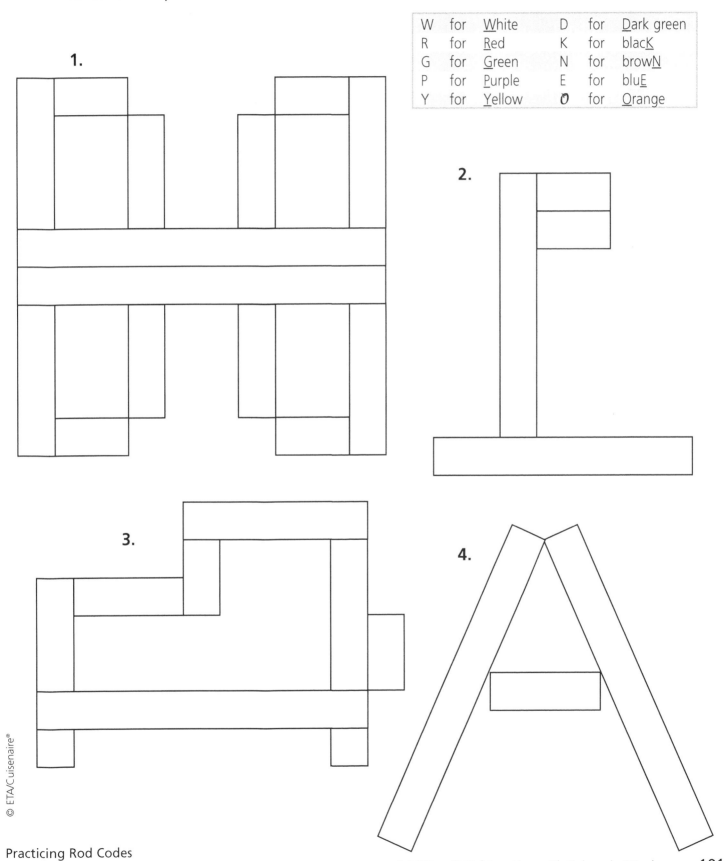

1.

2.

3.

4.

© ETA/Cuisenaire®

Name _____ Date _____

1. Put the rod for each code on the strip.
2. Color its length.
3. Check your answers with the rods.

W	for	White	D	for	Dark green
R	for	Red	K	for	blacK
G	for	Green	N	for	browN
P	for	Purple	E	for	bluE
Y	for	Yellow	O	for	Orange

Example:

D

1. P

2. K

3. R

4. Y

5. G

6. O

7. N

8. E

Matching Codes and Rods
Worksheet 1

Name _____ Date _____

1. Put the rod for each code on the strip.
2. Color its length.
3. Check your answers with the rods.

Example:

K

1. P

2. W

3. D

4. R

5. O

6. N

7. E

8. G

9. Y

© ETA/Cuisenaire®

Name _____ Date _____

1. Cover each rod picture with white rods.
2. Circle the number of white rods used.
3. Color the rod pictures with the correct colors.

Example:

$\boxed{}$ 3 (4) 5 6

1. $\boxed{}$ 5 6 7 8

2. $\boxed{}$ 7 8 9 10

3. $\boxed{}$ 2 3 4 5

4. $\boxed{}$ 2 3 4 5

5. $\boxed{}$ 7 8 9 10

6. $\boxed{}$ 1 2 3 4

7. $\boxed{}$ 5 6 7 8

8. $\boxed{}$ 6 7 8 9

Matching Rods and Numerals
Worksheet 1

Name _____ Date _____

1. Cover each rod picture with white rods.
2. Draw a line from each rod picture to the number of white rods that cover it.
3. Color the rod pictures with the correct colors.

Example:

1

1.   2

2.   3

3.   4

4.   5

5.   6

6.   7

7.   8

8.   9

9.   10

Name _____ Date _____

1. Find the rod that matches each train of white rods.
2. Color the length with the correct rod color.
3. Check your answers with the rods.

Example:

6W ▮▮▮▮▮▮□□□□□□□□□□

1. 3W □□□□□□□□□□□□□□□□
2. 8W □□□□□□□□□□□□□□□□
3. 5W □□□□□□□□□□□□□□□□
4. 2W □□□□□□□□□□□□□□□□
5. 4W □□□□□□□□□□□□□□□□
6. 9W □□□□□□□□□□□□□□□□
7. 7W □□□□□□□□□□□□□□□□
8. 10W □□□□□□□□□□□□□□□□

Coloring Rod Lengths
Worksheet 1

Name _____ Date _____

1. Find the rod that matches each train of white rods.
2. Color the length with the correct rod color.
3. Check your answers with the rods.

Example:

4W

1. 7W

2. 1W

3. 3W

4. 5W

5. 10W

6. 2W

7. 8W

8. 6W

Name _____ Date _____

1. Color the correct length for each rod code.
2. Write the number of white rods that match the rod.
3. Check your answers with the rods.

W	for	White	D	for	Dark green
R	for	Red	K	for	blacK
G	for	Green	N	for	browN
P	for	Purple	E	for	bluE
Y	for	Yellow	O	for	Orange

Example: ──────────────────────

G **3W**
number of white rods

1. O _____
number of white rods

2. K _____
number of white rods

3. W _____
number of white rods

4. E _____
number of white rods

5. R _____
number of white rods

6. N _____
number of white rods

7. Y _____
number of white rods

8. P _____
number of white rods

9. D _____
number of white rods

Matching Codes and Lengths
Worksheet

© ETA/Cuisenaire®

Name _____ Date _____

1. Write the code for the rod that matches each train of white rods.
2. Say the words that you make with the rod codes.

Example:

2W	9W	6W
R	E	D

1.

3W	10W	10W	6W

2.

6W	10W	3W

3.

3W	10W

4.

6W	10W	1W	8W

5.

2W	10W	4W	9W

6.

5W	10W	5W	10W

7.

4W	10W	1W	9W	2W

Name _____ Date _____

1. Write the code for the rod that matches each train of white rods.
2. Say the words that you make with the rod codes.

1.

2W	10W	6W

2.

9W	8W	6W

3.

7W	9W	9W	4W

4.

3W	2W	10W	1W

5.

4W	10W	8W	6W

6.

3W	2W	9W	9W	8W

7.

4W	9W	9W	7W

8.

10W	1W	8W	9W	2W

Name _____ Date _____

1. Write the code for the rod that matches each train of white rods.
2. Say the words that you make with the rod codes.

1.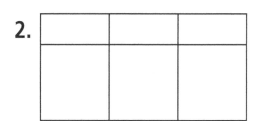

2.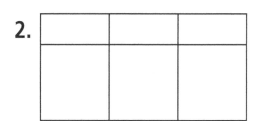

3.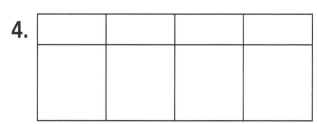

4.

5.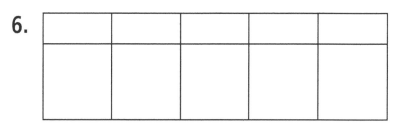

6.

7.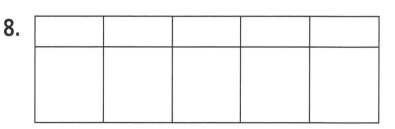

8.

Matching Numerals and Codes
Master

Name _____ Date _____

1. Find one rod that matches each train of red rods.
2. Color the length with the correct rod color.

Example:

3R

1. **1R**

2. **4R**

3. **2R**

4. **5R**

5. **3R**

3. Then find these words.

1R	5R	3R

2R	5R	5R	1R

Name _____ Date _____

1. Find a rod that is less than the rod shown.
2. Color the length of the rod that you have found.

Example:

1.

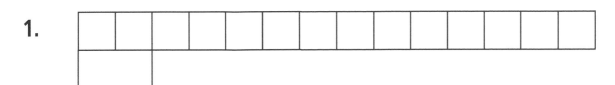

2.

3.

4.

5.

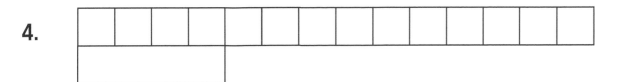

Name _____ Date _____

1. Find the rod that matches this rod picture.
2. Color this rod picture.

3. Circle and color all the pictures of rods that are less than this rod.

Addition & Subtraction with Cuisenaire® Rods

Practicing "Less Than"
Worksheet 2

Name _____ Date _____

1. Find the rod that matches this rod picture.
2. Color this rod picture.

3. Circle and color all the pictures of rods that are less than this rod.

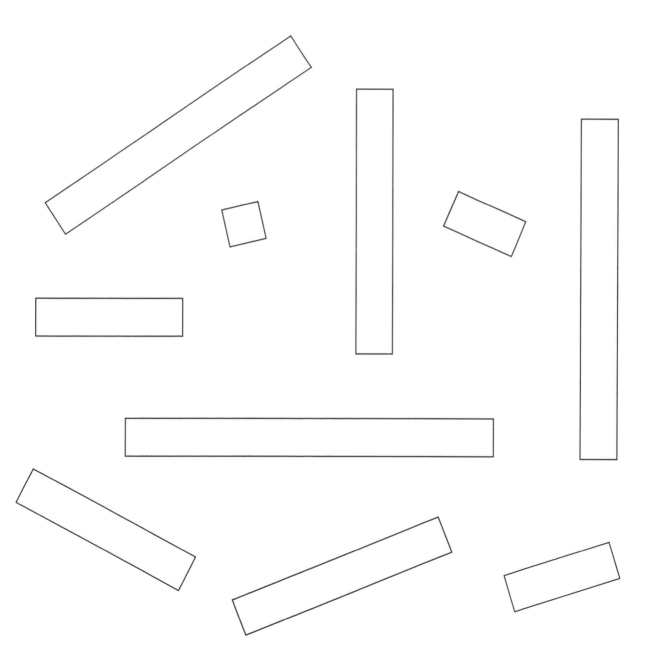

Practicing "Less Than"
Worksheet 3

Name _____ Date _____

1. Choose a rod and color its length on the strip.
2. Circle all the pictures of rods that are less than this rod.
3. Color the rods the correct colors.

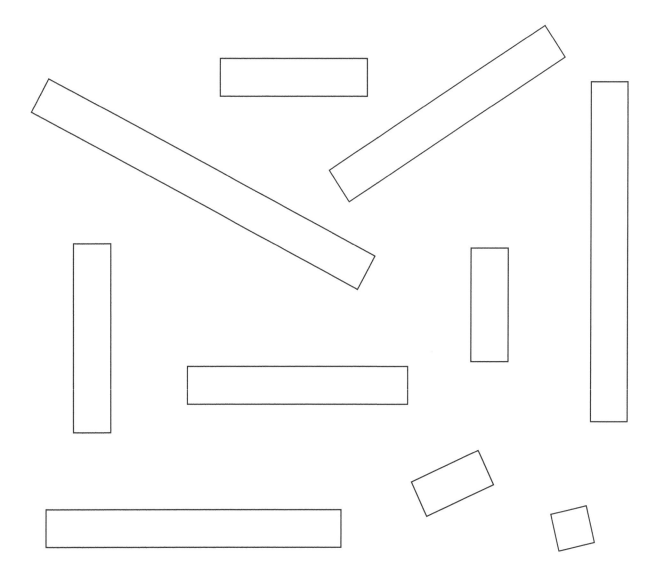

Addition & Subtraction with Cuisenaire® Rods

Practicing "Less Than"
Master

Name _____ Date _____

1. Find a rod that is greater than the rod shown.
2. Color the length of the rod that you have found.

Example:

1.

2.

3.

4.

5.

Name _____ Date _____

1. Find the rod that matches this rod picture.
2. Color this rod picture.

3. Circle and color all the pictures of rods that are greater than this rod.

Addition & Subtraction with Cuisenaire® Rods

Practicing "Greater Than"
Worksheet 2

Name _____ Date _____

1. Find the rod that matches this rod picture.
2. Color this rod picture.

3. Circle and color all the pictures of rods that are greater than this rod.

Name _____ Date _____

1. Choose a rod and color its length on the strip.
2. Circle all the pitures of rods that are greater than this rod.
3. Color the rods the correct colors.

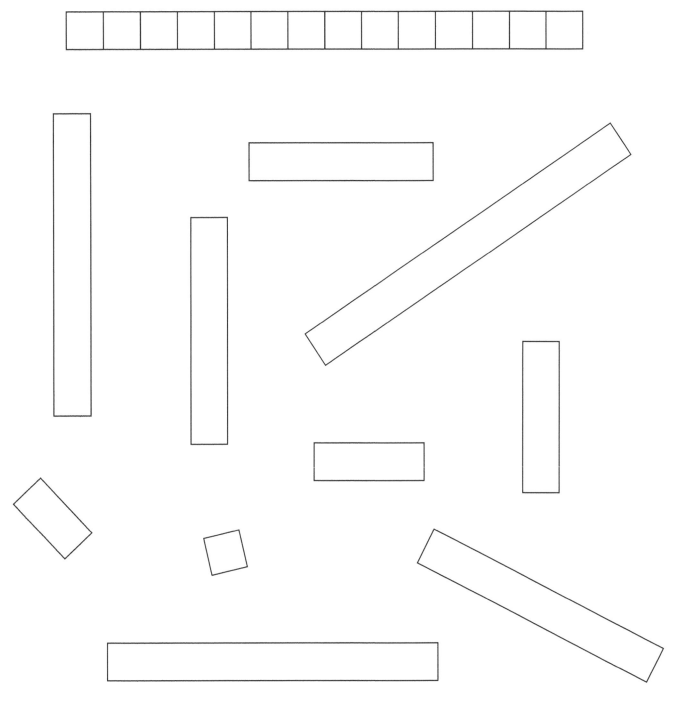

Addition & Subtraction with Cuisenaire® Rods

Practicing "Greater Than"
Master

© ETA/Cuisenaire®

Name _____ Date _____

1. Write the correct sign, < (less than) or > (greater than).
2. Color the rod pictures the correct colors.

Example:

[ ]   **<**   [ ]

1. [ ] ____ [ ]

2. [ ] ____ [ ]

3. [ ] ____ [ ]

4. [ ] ____ [ ]

5. [ ] ____ [ ]

6. [ ] ____ [ ]

Name _____ Date _____

1. Find a rod to complete each inequality.
2. Color the length of the rod that you have found.

Example:

>

1.

<

2.

>

3.

<

4.

>

5.

>

6.

>

Practicing Inequality Signs
Worksheet 2

© ETA/Cuisenaire®

Name _____ Date _____

1. Write the correct sign, < (less than) or > (greater than).
2. Check your answers with rods.

Examples:

$$3 \underline{\ <\ } 7 \qquad 7 \underline{\ >\ } 3$$

1. 5 ___ 9

2. 9 ___ 5

3. 7 ___ 4

4. 4 ___ 7

5. 6 ___ 7

6. 7 ___ 6

7. 10 ___ 8

8. 8 ___ 10

9. 2 ___ 1

10. 1 ___ 2

Name _____ Date _____

1. ☐☐☐☐☐☐☐☐☐☐☐☐☐☐☐☐☐

2. ☐☐☐☐☐☐☐☐☐☐☐☐☐☐☐☐☐

3. ☐☐☐☐☐☐☐☐☐☐☐☐☐☐☐☐☐

4. ☐☐☐☐☐☐☐☐☐☐☐☐☐☐☐☐☐

5. ☐☐☐☐☐☐☐☐☐☐☐☐☐☐☐☐☐

6. ☐☐☐☐☐☐☐☐☐☐☐☐☐☐☐☐☐

7. ☐☐☐☐☐☐☐☐☐☐☐☐☐☐☐☐☐

8. ☐☐☐☐☐☐☐☐☐☐☐☐☐☐☐☐☐

9. ☐☐☐☐☐☐☐☐☐☐☐☐☐☐☐☐☐

10. ☐☐☐☐☐☐☐☐☐☐☐☐☐☐☐☐☐

Making Trains
Master

Name _____ Date _____

1. Find the rod that matches each rod picture.
2. Find all the two-car trains that match this rod.
3. Color the pictures of the trains.

1.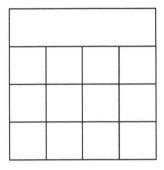

2.

3.

Name _____ Date _____

1. Find the rod that matches each rod picture.
2. Find all the two-car trains that match this rod.
3. Color the pictures of the trains.

1.

2.

Finding All Two-Car Trains
Worksheet 2

© ETA/Cuisenaire®

Name _____ Date _____

Use the rod codes to write the plus story for each train picture.

Example:

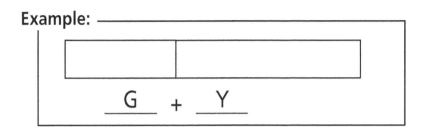

__G__ + __Y__

1.

_____ + _____

2.

_____ + _____

3.

_____ + _____

4.

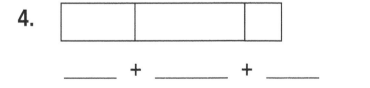

_____ + _____ + _____

5.

_____ + _____ + _____

Name _____ Date _____

Use the rod codes to write the plus story for each train picture.

Example: ──────────────────────

P + Y
_____

1. [train picture] _____

2. [train picture] _____

3. [train picture] _____

4. [train picture] _____

5. [train picture] _____

6. [train picture] _____

Name _____ Date _____

Color the train picture for each plus story.

Example:

P + Y

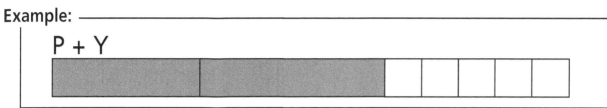

G + D

1.
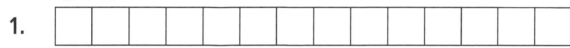

E + W

2.
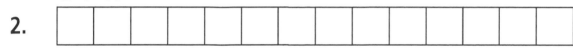

R + K

3.
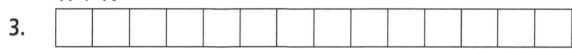

Y + G

4.
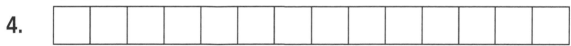

D + P

5.

Name _____ Date _____

Color the train picture for each plus story.

K + R

1.

G + P

2.

N + W

3.

D + G

4.

R + N

5.

Y + Y

6.

Name _____ Date _____

1. Find the rod that matches each train.
2. Color the rod picture.
3. Write the plus story.

Example:

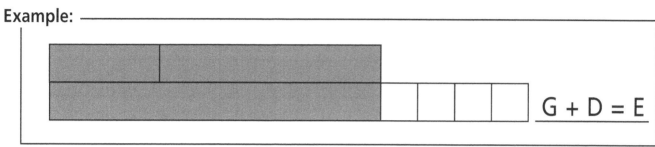

$G + D = E$

1.

_____

2.

_____

3.

_____

4.

_____

Name _____ Date _____

1. Find the rod that matches each train.
2. Color the rod picture.
3. Write the plus story.

1. 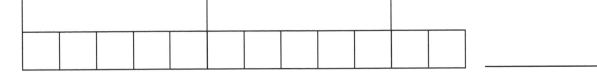 _____

2. 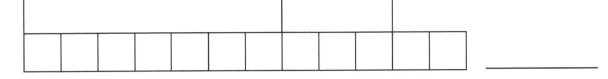 _____

3. 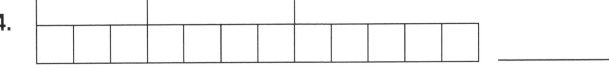 _____

4. 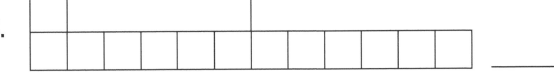 _____

5. 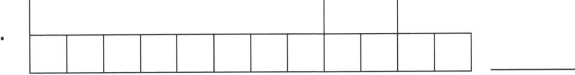 _____

6. _____

Name _____ Date _____

1. Color the train picture for each plus story.
2. Find and color the length that matches each train.
3. Use codes to write the complete plus story.

Example:

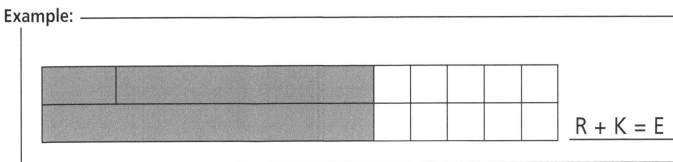

R + K = E

N + R

1.

_____

G + Y

2.

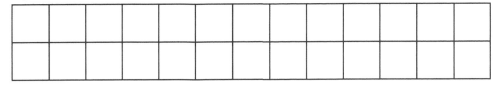

_____

P + R

3.

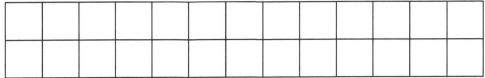

_____

R + D

4.

_____

Name _____ Date _____

1. Color the train picture for each plus story.
2. Find and color the length that matches each train.
3. Use codes to write the complete plus story.

Y + P

1. 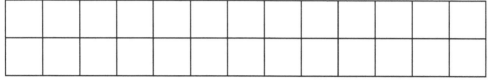 _____

K + W

2. 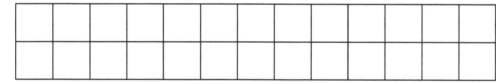 _____

G + D

3.  _____

R + Y

4. _____

R + N

5. _____

Completing Plus Stories
Worksheet 2

© ETA/Cuisenaire®

Name _____ Date _____

1. Find all the trains that match the rod picture.
2. Color each train.
3. Write plus stories for your trains.

Example: ─────────────────────────────────

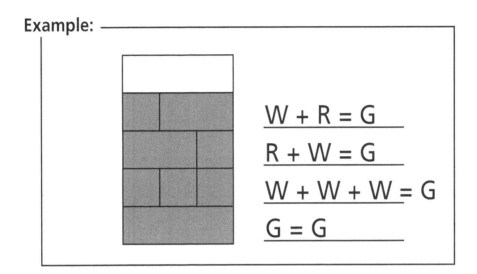

$$W + R = G$$
$$R + W = G$$
$$W + W + W = G$$
$$G = G$$

_____

_____

_____

_____

_____

_____

_____

_____

Name _____ Date _____

1. Find lots of different trains that match the orange rod.
2. Color each train.
3. Write plus stories for your trains.

_____

_____

_____

_____

_____

_____

_____

_____

_____

_____

_____

_____

_____

_____

Name _____ Date _____

1. Find a rod that matches both trains.
2. Color its length.
3. Write plus stories for each train.

Example:

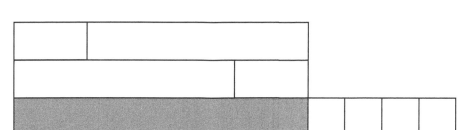

$$R + D = N$$
$$D + R = N$$

1.

_____

_____

2.

_____

_____

3.

_____

_____

Name _____ Date _____

1. Find another plus story using the same three rods.
2. Use codes to write the new plus story.

Example:

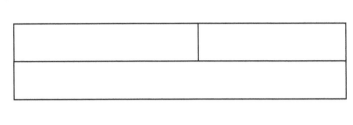

Y + P = E
P + Y = E

1.

R + W = G

_____

2.

D + R = N

_____

3.

W + N = E

_____

4.

G + K = O

_____

Using the Same Three Rods
Worksheet

Name _____ Date _____

1. Color the train picture for each plus story.
2. Find and color the length that matches each train.
3. Write the number sentence.

Example:

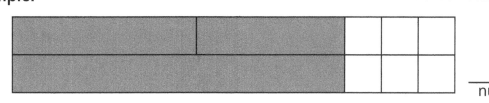

$$5 + 4 = 9$$
number sentence

G + R

1.

_____
number sentence

D + G

2.

_____
number sentence

N + W

3.

_____
number sentence

K + G

4.

_____
number sentence

W + E

5.

_____
number sentence

P + P

6.

_____
number sentence

Changing Rod Stories to Number Sentences
Worksheet

Name _____ Date _____

1. Find the rod that matches each train.
2. Color its length.
3. Write an addition sentence.

Example: ───────────────────────────────

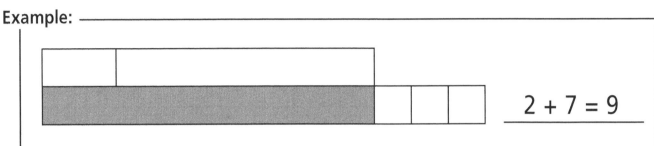

2 + 7 = 9

1.

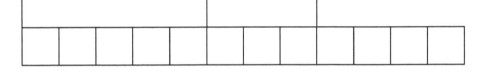

addition sentence

2.

addition sentence

3.

addition sentence

4.

addition sentence

5.

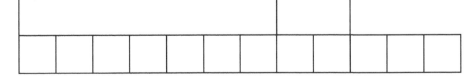

addition sentence

Writing Addition Sentences
Worksheet 1

Name _____ Date _____

1. Find the rod that matches each train.
2. Color its length.
3. Write an addition sentence.

1.

_____
addition sentence

2.

_____
addition sentence

3.

_____
addition sentence

4.

_____
addition sentence

5.

_____
addition sentence

6.

_____
addition sentence

Name _____ Date _____

1. Color each train.
2. Find the rod that matches the train and color its length.
3. Write an addition sentence.

Example:

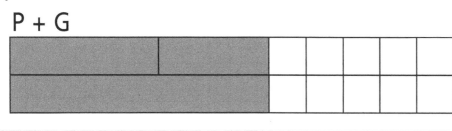

P + G

4 + 3 = 7

W + Y

1.

addition sentence

D + R

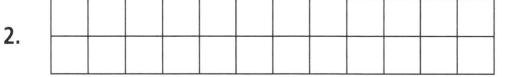

2.

addition sentence

G + G

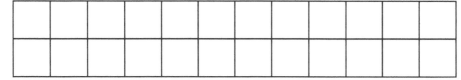

3.

addition sentence

P + D

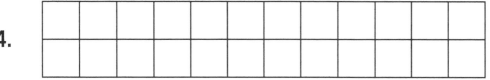

4.

addition sentence

Practicing Addition Sentences
Worksheet 1

© ETA/Cuisenaire®

Name _____ Date _____

1. Color each train.
2. Find the rod that matches the train and color its length.
3. Write an addition sentence.

G + R

1.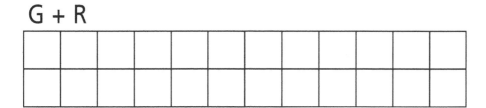

_____
addition sentence

Y + P

2.

_____
addition sentence

R + W

3.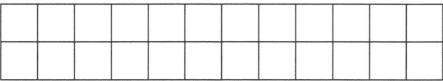

_____
addition sentence

P + D

4.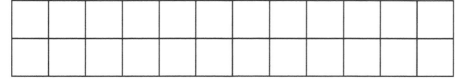

_____
addition sentence

K + R

5.

_____
addition sentence

Name _____ Date _____

1. Write the code for a train with two cars.
2. Color the train.
3. Find and color the length that matches the train.
4. Write an addition sentence.

1.

_____

addition sentence

2.

_____

addition sentence

3.

_____

addition sentence

4.

_____

addition sentence

5.

_____

addition sentence

Name _____ Date _____

1. Color a picture of the train to match the number story.
2. Color the single length that matches each train.
3. Complete the addition sentence.

Example:

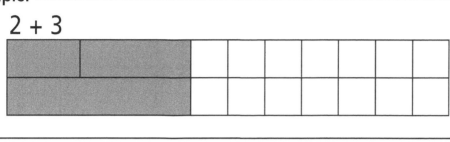

2 + 3

$$2 + 3 = 5$$
addition sentence

1.

5 + 4

$$5 + 4 = \underline{\hspace{2cm}}$$
addition sentence

2.

1 + 7

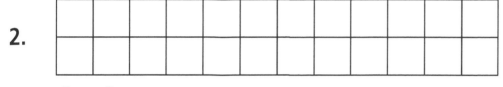

$$1 + 7 = \underline{\hspace{2cm}}$$
addition sentence

3.

3 + 6

$$3 + 6 = \underline{\hspace{2cm}}$$
addition sentence

4.

8 + 2

$$8 + 2 = \underline{\hspace{2cm}}$$
addition sentence

5.

6 + 4

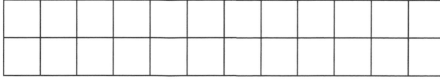

$$6 + 4 = \underline{\hspace{2cm}}$$
addition sentence

Name _____ Date _____

1. Color a picture of the train to match the number story.
2. Color the single length that matches each train.
3. Complete the addition sentence.

3 + 4

1.

3 + 4 = _____
addition sentence

5 + 5

2.

5 + 5 = _____
addition sentence

4 + 1

3.

4 + 1 = _____
addition sentence

2 + 6

4.

2 + 6 = _____
addition sentence

5 + 2

5.

5 + 2 = _____
addition sentence

7 + 3

6.

7 + 3 = _____
addition sentence

Finding Sums
Worksheet 2

© ETA/Cuisenaire®

Name _____ Date _____

1. Write a number story for addition.
2. Color a picture of the train to match the story.
3. Color the single length that matches each train.
4. Write the addition sentence.

1.

_____
addition sentence

2.

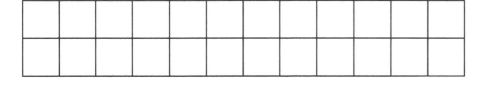

_____
addition sentence

3.

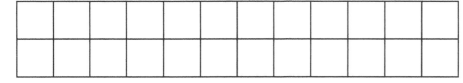

_____
addition sentence

4.

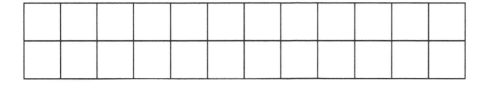

_____
addition sentence

5.

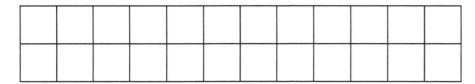

_____
addition sentence

Finding Sums
Master

Name _____ Date _____

1. Use rods on the number lines to help find the sums.
2. Complete the addition sentences.

Example:

3 + 6 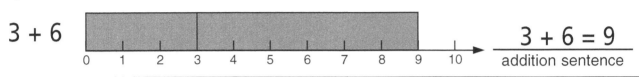   3 + 6 = 9
       0 1 2 3 4 5 6 7 8 9 10   _____
                                          addition sentence

1. 2 + 4
0 1 2 3 4 5 6 7 8 9 10
2 + 4 = _____
addition sentence

2. 6 + 2
0 1 2 3 4 5 6 7 8 9 10
6 + 2 = _____
addition sentence

3. 5 + 3
0 1 2 3 4 5 6 7 8 9 10
5 + 3 = _____
addition sentence

4. 4 + 5
0 1 2 3 4 5 6 7 8 9 10
4 + 5 = _____
addition sentence

5. 1 + 9
0 1 2 3 4 5 6 7 8 9 10
1 + 9 = _____
addition sentence

6. 2 + 7
0 1 2 3 4 5 6 7 8 9 10
2 + 7 = _____
addition sentence

7. 7 + 3
0 1 2 3 4 5 6 7 8 9 10
7 + 3 = _____
addition sentence

Using a Number Line to Add
Worksheet 1

Name _____ Date _____

1. Use rods on the number lines to help find the sums.
2. Complete the addition sentences.

1. 2 + 5
0 1 2 3 4 5 6 7 8 9 10
$$2 + 5 =$$ _____
addition sentence

2. 5 + 3
0 1 2 3 4 5 6 7 8 9 10
$$5 + 3 =$$ _____
addition sentence

3. 7 + 2
0 1 2 3 4 5 6 7 8 9 10
$$7 + 2 =$$ _____
addition sentence

4. 4 + 4
0 1 2 3 4 5 6 7 8 9 10
$$4 + 4 =$$ _____
addition sentence

5. 1 + 6
0 1 2 3 4 5 6 7 8 9 10
$$1 + 6 =$$ _____
addition sentence

6. 3 + 4
0 1 2 3 4 5 6 7 8 9 10
$$3 + 4 =$$ _____
addition sentence

7. 6 + 3
0 1 2 3 4 5 6 7 8 9 10
$$6 + 3 =$$ _____
addition sentence

8. 9 + 1
0 1 2 3 4 5 6 7 8 9 10
$$9 + 1 =$$ _____
addition sentence

9. 2 + 8
0 1 2 3 4 5 6 7 8 9 10
$$2 + 8 =$$ _____
addition sentence

Using a Number Line to Add
Worksheet 2

Addition & Subtraction with Cuisenaire® Rods

Name _____ Date _____

1. Write some number stories for addition.
2. Use rods on the number lines to help find the sums.
3. Write a complete addition sentence for each number story.

1. _____ 0 1 2 3 4 5 6 7 8 9 10 → _____
                                                    addition sentence

2. _____ 0 1 2 3 4 5 6 7 8 9 10 → _____
                                                    addition sentence

3. _____ 0 1 2 3 4 5 6 7 8 9 10 → _____
                                                    addition sentence

4. _____ 0 1 2 3 4 5 6 7 8 9 10 → _____
                                                    addition sentence

5. _____ 0 1 2 3 4 5 6 7 8 9 10 → _____
                                                    addition sentence

6. _____ 0 1 2 3 4 5 6 7 8 9 10 → _____
                                                    addition sentence

7. _____ 0 1 2 3 4 5 6 7 8 9 10 → _____
                                                    addition sentence

8. _____ 0 1 2 3 4 5 6 7 8 9 10 → _____
                                                    addition sentence

9. _____ 0 1 2 3 4 5 6 7 8 9 10 → _____
                                                    addition sentence

Addition & Subtraction with Cuisenaire® Rods

Using a Number Line to Add
Master

Name _____ Date _____

1. Stand rods on end to build a plus table.

+	W	R	G	P	Y	D	K	N	E
W									
R									
G									
P									
Y									
D									
K									
N									
E									

2. Use numerals to make an addition table.

+	1	2	3	4	5	6	7	8	9
1									
2									
3									
4									
5									
6									
7									
8									
9									

Building an Addition Table for Sums Through 10
Worksheet

Name _____ Date _____

1. Find the sums.
2. Check your answers with rods, using the number line below.

1. 3 + 5 = _____   **2.** 6 + 3 = _____

3. 1 + 7 = _____   **4.** 4 + 3 = _____

5. 2 + 2 = _____   **6.** 2 + 3 = _____

7. 5 + 5 = _____   **8.** 1 + 2 = _____

9. 3 + 7 = _____   **10.** 4 + 4 = _____

11. 2 + 8 = _____   **12.** 6 + 1 = _____

13. 3 + 3 = _____   **14.** 5 + 4 = _____

15. 6 + 4 = _____   **16.** 7 + 2 = _____

Challenge: ## Challenge:

17. 4 + 0 = _____   **18.** 0 + 9 = _____

Checking Sums Through 10
Worksheet 1

Name _____ Date _____

1. Find the sums.
2. Check your answers with rods, using the number line below.

1. 2 + 4 = _____

2. 1 + 3 = _____

3. 3 + 2 = _____

4. 4 + 2 = _____

5. 4 + 1 = _____

6. 1 + 4 = _____

7. 1 + 6 = _____

8. 1 + 8 = _____

9. 2 + 5 = _____

10. 3 + 6 = _____

11. 3 + 4 = _____

12. 2 + 6 = _____

13. 8 + 2 = _____

14. 5 + 5 = _____

15. 4 + 6 = _____

16. 9 + 1 = _____

17. 3 + 0 = _____

18. 0 + 7 = _____

```
 |---|---|---|---|---|---|---|---|---|---|--->
 0   1   2   3   4   5   6   7   8   9   10
```

Name _____ Date _____

1. Find the missing rod.
2. Draw and color the completed picture.

Example:

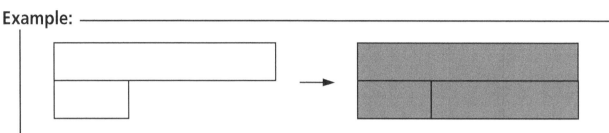

1.

2.

3.

4.

5.

Practicing Missing Addends
Worksheet 1

Name _____ Date _____

1. Find the missing rod.
2. Draw and color the completed picture.
3. Use codes to write a completed rod story.

Example:

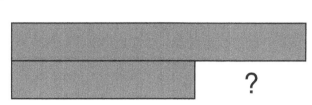

Y + G = N

1. ? _____

2. ? _____

3. ? _____

4. ? _____

5. ? _____

6. ? _____

© ETA/Cuisenaire®

Name _____ Date _____

1. Color the rod picture for the missing rod story.
2. Use numerals to write the missing addend sentence.
3. Write the complete addition sentence.

Example:

G + __ = Y 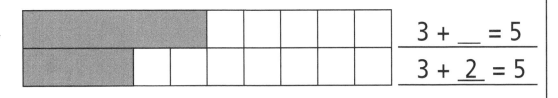 $\dfrac{3 + \underline{} = 5}{3 + \underline{2} = 5}$

1. R + __ = O 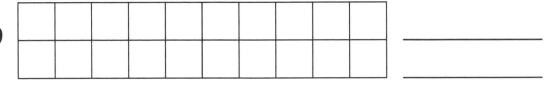 _____

_____

2. K + __ = E 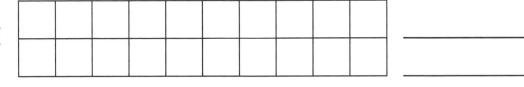 _____

_____

3. P + __ = N 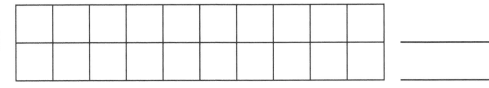 _____

_____

4. W + __ = D  _____

_____

5. P + __ = K  _____

_____

Name _____ Date _____

1. Color the correct rods to match the numerals.
2. Find and color the missing rod.
3. Write the complete addition sentence.

Example:

$4 + \_\_ = 7$

$\underline{4 + 3 = 7}$

1. $5 + \_\_ = 10$ _____

2. $2 + \_\_ = 6$ _____

3. $1 + \_\_ = 10$ _____

4. $3 + \_\_ = 8$ _____

5. $6 + \_\_ = 9$ _____

6. $2 + \_\_ = 7$ _____

Completing Missing Addend Sentences
Worksheet 1

Addition & Subtraction with Cuisenaire® Rods

Name _____ Date _____

1. Color the correct rods to match the numerals.
2. Find and color the missing rod.
3. Write the complete addition sentence.

1. $2 + \underline{} = 8$ 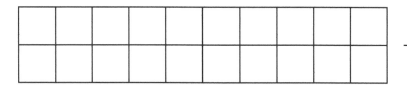 _____

2. $5 + \underline{} = 7$ 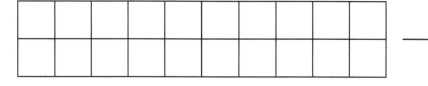 _____

3. $1 + \underline{} = 10$ 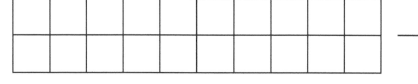 _____

4. $7 + \underline{} = 9$  _____

5. $3 + \underline{} = 6$ 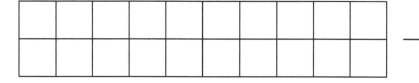 _____

6. $5 + \underline{} = 8$ 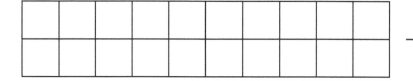 _____

7. $4 + \underline{} = 10$  _____

Name _____ Date _____

1. Complete the missing addend sentences.
2. Check your answers on the grid below.

1. $3 + \underline{\hspace{1cm}} = 9$

2. $7 + \underline{\hspace{1cm}} = 8$

3. $1 + \underline{\hspace{1cm}} = 6$

4. $2 + \underline{\hspace{1cm}} = 4$

5. $9 + \underline{\hspace{1cm}} = 10$

6. $3 + \underline{\hspace{1cm}} = 10$

7. $4 + \underline{\hspace{1cm}} = 9$

8. $1 + \underline{\hspace{1cm}} = 8$

9. $2 + \underline{\hspace{1cm}} = 6$

10. $4 + \underline{\hspace{1cm}} = 6$

11. $6 + \underline{\hspace{1cm}} = 7$

12. $2 + \underline{\hspace{1cm}} = 7$

13. $3 + \underline{\hspace{1cm}} = 10$

14. $4 + \underline{\hspace{1cm}} = 8$

Challenge:
15. $4 + \underline{\hspace{1cm}} = 4$

Challenge:
16. $0 + \underline{\hspace{1cm}} = 8$

Name _____ Date _____

1. Color the rod picture for the two rods shown.
2. Find and color the missing rod.

Example:

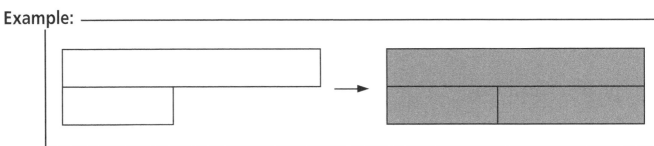

1.

2.

3.

4.

5.

Finding the Difference
Worksheet

Name _____ Date _____

1. Listen to the teacher tell you a minus story.
2. Color the rods described.
3. Complete the rod picture.

1.

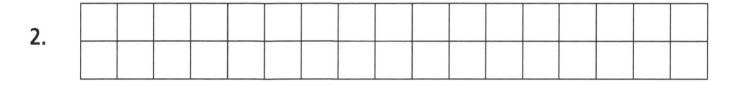

2.

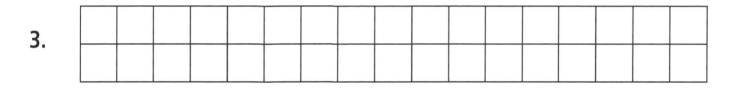

3.

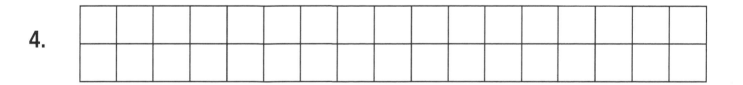

4.

5.

6.

Finding the Difference
Master

Name _____ Date _____

1. Color the rods shown.
2. Use rod codes to write the minus story.

Example:

D – P
_____

1.

_____

2.

_____

3.

_____

4.

_____

Name _____ Date _____

1. Write the minus story for each rod picture.
2. Find the missing rod.
3. Write the complete minus story.

Example:

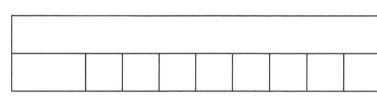

$O - R$ _____ $O - R = N$ _____

1.

_____   _____

2.

_____   _____

3.

_____   _____

4.

_____   _____

5.

_____   _____

Name _____ Date _____

1. Make some rod pictures showing minus stories.
2. Write the minus story for each rod picture.
3. Find the missing rod.
4. Write the complete minus story.

1.  _____ _____

2. _____ _____

3. 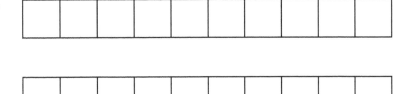 _____ _____

4. _____ _____

5. _____ _____

6. _____ _____

Name _____ Date _____

1. Color the minus story.
2. Write the subtraction story.
3. Write the complete subtraction sentence.

Example:

Y – G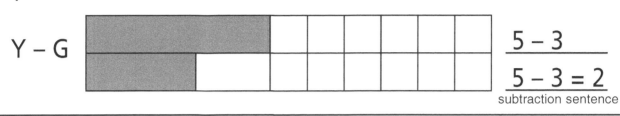

$$5 - 3$$
$$\overline{5 - 3 = 2}$$
subtraction sentence

1. D – R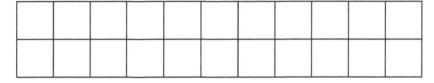

_____
_____
subtraction sentence

2. E – G

_____
_____
subtraction sentence

3. O – Y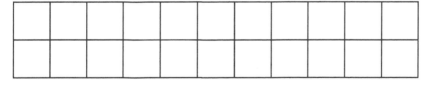

_____
_____
subtraction sentence

4. N – P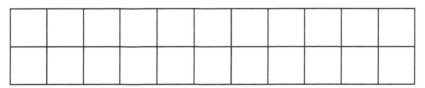

_____
_____
subtraction sentence

Writing Subtraction Sentences
Worksheet 1

Name _____ Date _____

1. Color the minus story.
2. Write the subtraction story.
3. Write the complete subtraction sentence.

Example:

K – P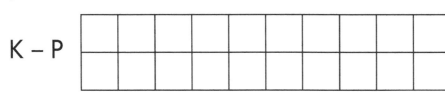

$$\frac{7-4}{7-4=3}$$
subtraction sentence

1. P – W

_____
_____
subtraction sentence

2. D – P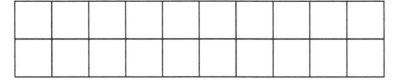

_____
_____
subtraction sentence

3. O – R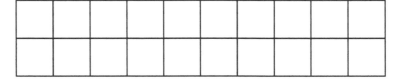

_____
_____
subtraction sentence

4. K – G

_____
_____
subtraction sentence

5. E – Y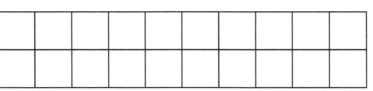

_____
_____
subtraction sentence

Writing Subtraction Sentences
Worksheet 2

Name _____ Date _____

1. Write a minus story for rods.
2. Color your minus story.
3. Write the number story and the complete subtraction sentence.

1. _____

_____
_____
subtraction sentence

2. _____

_____
_____
subtraction sentence

3. _____

_____
_____
subtraction sentence

4. _____

_____
_____
subtraction sentence

5. _____

_____
_____
subtraction sentence

6. _____

_____
_____
subtraction sentence

Writing Subtraction Sentences
Master

Name _____ Date _____

1. Use rods on the number line to help find the difference.
2. Write the complete subtraction sentence.

Example:

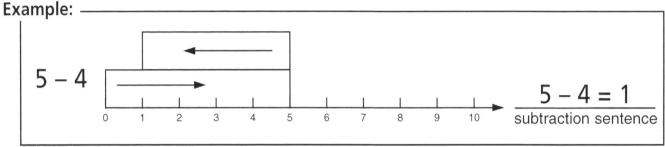

$$5 - 4$$

$$\frac{5 - 4 = 1}{\text{subtraction sentence}}$$

1. $8 - 6$

0 1 2 3 4 5 6 7 8 9 10

_____
subtraction sentence

2. $7 - 1$

0 1 2 3 4 5 6 7 8 9 10

_____
subtraction sentence

3. $6 - 4$

0 1 2 3 4 5 6 7 8 9 10

_____
subtraction sentence

4. $9 - 2$

0 1 2 3 4 5 6 7 8 9 10

_____
subtraction sentence

5. $8 - 3$

0 1 2 3 4 5 6 7 8 9 10

_____
subtraction sentence

6. $10 - 7$

0 1 2 3 4 5 6 7 8 9 10

_____
subtraction sentence

Using a Number Line to Subtract
Worksheet 1

Name _____ Date _____

1. Use rods on the number line to help find the difference.
2. Write the complete subtraction sentence.

Example:

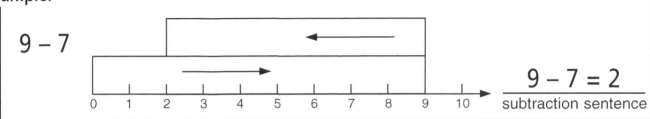

9 – 7

$\underline{9 – 7 = 2}$
subtraction sentence

1. 7 – 3

0 1 2 3 4 5 6 7 8 9 10

_____
subtraction sentence

2. 5 – 2

0 1 2 3 4 5 6 7 8 9 10

_____
subtraction sentence

3. 8 – 1

0 1 2 3 4 5 6 7 8 9 10

_____
subtraction sentence

4. 10 – 4

0 1 2 3 4 5 6 7 8 9 10

_____
subtraction sentence

5. 8 – 5

0 1 2 3 4 5 6 7 8 9 10

_____
subtraction sentence

6. 9 – 6

0 1 2 3 4 5 6 7 8 9 10

_____
subtraction sentence

Name _____ Date _____

1. Write a minus story using numbers through 10.
2. Use the rods on the number lines to help find the differences.
3. Write the complete subtraction sentence.

1. _____
0 1 2 3 4 5 6 7 8 9 10   _____ subtraction sentence

2. _____
0 1 2 3 4 5 6 7 8 9 10   _____ subtraction sentence

3. _____
0 1 2 3 4 5 6 7 8 9 10   _____ subtraction sentence

4. _____
0 1 2 3 4 5 6 7 8 9 10   _____ subtraction sentence

5. _____
0 1 2 3 4 5 6 7 8 9 10   _____ subtraction sentence

6. _____
0 1 2 3 4 5 6 7 8 9 10   _____ subtraction sentence

7. _____
0 1 2 3 4 5 6 7 8 9 10   _____ subtraction sentence

8. _____
0 1 2 3 4 5 6 7 8 9 10   _____ subtraction sentence

9. _____
0 1 2 3 4 5 6 7 8 9 10   _____ subtraction sentence

Using a Number Line to Subtract
Master

Name _____ Date _____

1. Color the rod picture to match the minus story.
2. Color the missing rod length.
3. Write the complete subtraction sentence.

Example:

6 – 4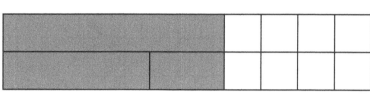

$$6 - 4 = 2$$
subtraction sentence

1. 5 – 1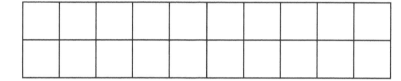

_____
subtraction sentence

2. 4 – 2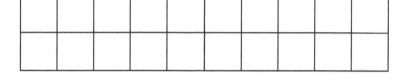

_____
subtraction sentence

3. 7 – 4

_____
subtraction sentence

4. 10 – 3

_____
subtraction sentence

5. 9 – 6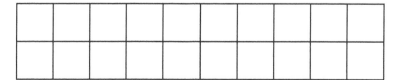

_____
subtraction sentence

Name _____ Date _____

1. Color the rod picture to match the minus story.
2. Color the missing rod length.
3. Write the complete subtraction sentence.

1. 5 – 3

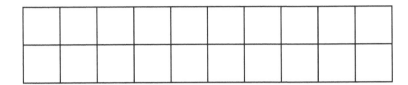

_____
subtraction sentence

2. 6 – 5

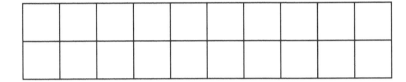

_____
subtraction sentence

3. 8 – 4

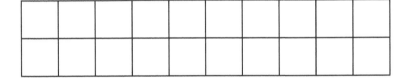

_____
subtraction sentence

4. 10 – 2

_____
subtraction sentence

5. 9 – 7

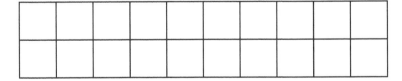

_____
subtraction sentence

6. 10 – 6

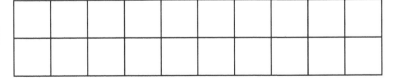

_____
subtraction sentence

Name _____ Date _____

1. Write a minus story using numbers through 10.
2. Color the rod picture to match your minus story.
3. Color the missing rod length.
4. Write the complete subtraction sentence.

1. _____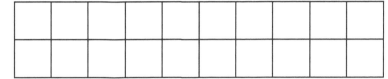

_____
subtraction sentence

2. _____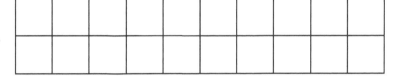

_____
subtraction sentence

3. _____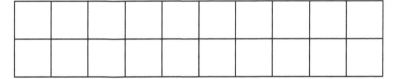

_____
subtraction sentence

4. _____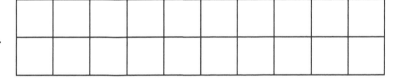

_____
subtraction sentence

5. _____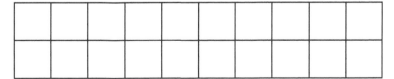

_____
subtraction sentence

6. _____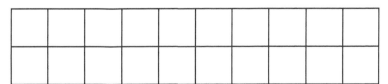

_____
subtraction sentence

Practicing Subtraction Sentences
Master

Name _____ Date _____

1. Write an addition sentence and a subtraction sentence for each rod picture.
2. Rearrange the same three rods to make one more addition sentence and one more subtraction sentence.
3. Write the two new sentences.

Example:

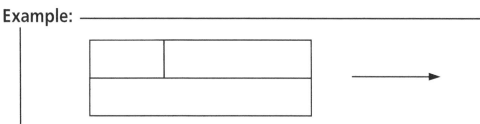

2 + 4 = 6

6 – 2 = 4

4 + 2 = 6

6 – 4 = 2

1.

_____   _____

_____   _____

addition sentences   subtraction sentences

2.

_____   _____

_____   _____

addition sentences   subtraction sentences

Writing Addition and Subtraction Sentences
Worksheet 1

Name _____ Date _____

1. Write an addition sentence and a subtraction sentence for each rod picture.
2. Rearrange the same three rods to make one more addition sentence and one more subtraction sentence.
3. Write the two new sentences.

1.

_____   _____

_____   _____

addition sentences   subtraction sentences

2.

_____   _____

_____   _____

addition sentences   subtraction sentences

3.

_____   _____

_____   _____

addition sentences   subtraction sentences

4.

_____   _____

_____   _____

addition sentences   subtraction sentences

5.

_____   _____

_____   _____

addition sentences   subtraction sentences

Name _____ Date _____

1. Write three more addition sentences or subtraction sentences that can be shown using the same three rods.
2. Use rods to help.

Example: ──────────────────────────────

1 + 8 = 9

8 + 1 = 9

9 – 1 = 8

9 – 8 = 1

1.   3 + 6 = 9

_____

_____

_____

2.   8 + 2 = 10

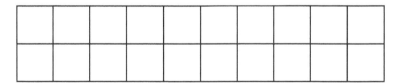

_____

_____

_____

3.   5 + 3 = 8

_____

_____

_____

Writing Addition and Subtraction Sentences
Worksheet 3

© ETA/Cuisenaire®

Name _____ Date _____

1. Match white rods with an orange rod plus another rod.
2. Write the plus story with codes and with numbers.

Example:

	Plus Story	Number Story
16 White Rods	O + ___D___	10 + ___6___

		Plus Story	Number Story
1.	19 White Rods	O + _____	10 + _____
2.	11 White Rods	O + _____	10 + _____
3.	15 White Rods	O + _____	10 + _____
4.	12 White Rods	O + _____	10 + _____
5.	17 White Rods	O + _____	10 + _____

Organizing Teen Numbers
Worksheet 1

Name _____ Date _____

1. Match white rods with an orange rod plus another rod.
2. Write the plus story with codes and with numbers.

		Plus Story	Number Story
1.	18 White Rods	O + _____	10 + _____
2.	20 White Rods	O + _____	10 + _____
3.	15 White Rods	O + _____	10 + _____
4.	12 White Rods	O + _____	10 + _____
5.	14 White Rods	O + _____	10 + _____
6.	13 White Rods	O + _____	10 + _____
7.	16 White Rods	O + _____	10 + _____

© ETA/Cuisenaire®

Name _____ Date _____

1. Color each train.
2. Match each train with an orange rod plus another rod.
3. Record your answers with rod codes.

Example:

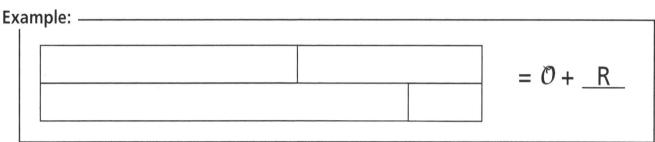

= $\mathcal{O}$ + R

1. = $\mathcal{O}$ + ____

2. = $\mathcal{O}$ + ____

3. = $\mathcal{O}$ + ____

4. = $\mathcal{O}$ + ____

5. = $\mathcal{O}$ + ____

6. = $\mathcal{O}$ + ____

Finding Sums Greater Than Orange
Worksheet 1

Name _____ Date _____

1. Color each train.
2. Match each train with an orange rod plus another rod.
3. Record your answers with rod codes.

Example:

Y + K = <u>O + R</u>

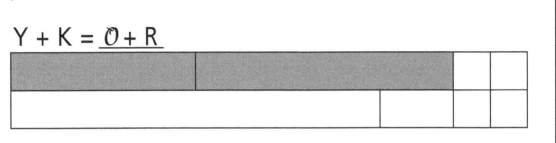

D + N = _____

1.

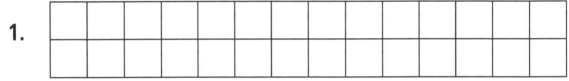

K + K = _____

2.

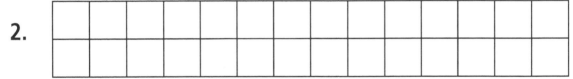

E + G = _____

3.

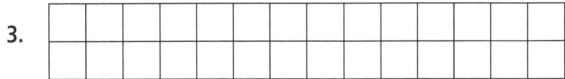

N + K = _____

4.

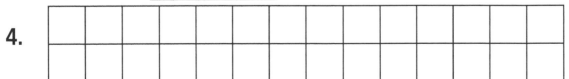

Finding Sums Greater Than Orange
Worksheet 2

© ETA/Cuisenaire®

Name _____ Date _____

1. Color each train.
2. Find the orange-plus train that will match.
3. Write the addition sentence and find the sum.

Example:

N + K $\underline{8} + \underline{7} = \underline{10} + \underline{5} = \underline{15}$

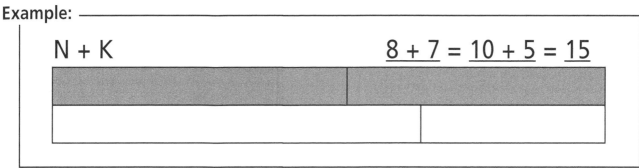

R + E   _____ + _____ = _____

1.

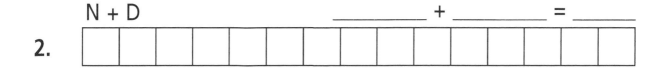

N + D   _____ + _____ = _____

2.

K + K   _____ + _____ = _____

3.

Y + D   _____ + _____ = _____

4.

G + E   _____ + _____ = _____

5.

Writing Addition Sentences for Sums Greater Than Orange
Worksheet 1

Name _____ Date _____

1. Color each train.
2. Find the orange plus train that will match.
3. Write the addition sentence and find the sum.

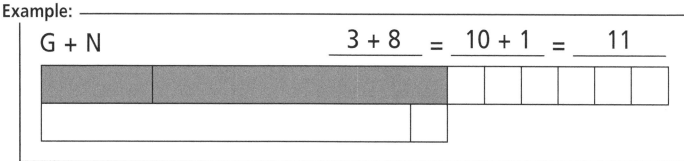

Example:

G + N   <u> 3 + 8 </u> = <u> 10 + 1 </u> = <u> 11 </u>

1. P + E   _____ = _____ = _____

2. Y + K   _____ = _____ = _____

3. E + N   _____ = _____ = _____

4. D + E   _____ = _____ = _____

Writing Addition Sentences for Sums Greater Than Orange
Worksheet 2

© ETA/Cuisenaire®

Name _____ Date _____

1. Find each sum.
2. Match each rod train with an orange-plus train.
3. Place rods on the grid to help.

Example:

| 8 + 3 | |
| 8 + 3 = 11 | |

1. 7 + 5 = _____

2. 4 + 8 = _____

3. 9 + 6 = _____

4. 7 + 7 = _____

5. 5 + 6 = _____

6. 5 + 9 = _____

7. 7 + 9 = _____

8. 9 + 7 = _____

9.   7
     + 8

10.   9
      + 9

11.   10
      + 2

12.   10
      + 8

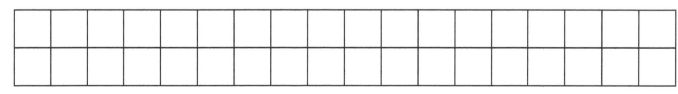

Writing Addition Sentences for Sums Greater Than Orange
Worksheet 3

Addition & Subtraction with Cuisenaire® Rods

Name _____ Date _____

1. Use rods on the number line to help find the sum.
2. Complete the addition sentence.

Example:

8 + 6

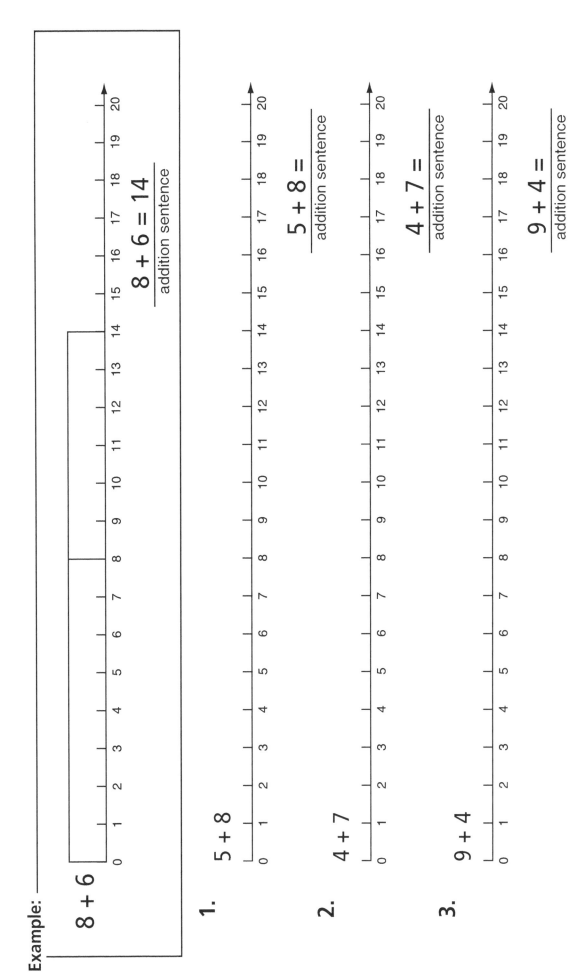

0 1 2 3 4 5 6 7 8 9 10 11 12 13 14 15 16 17 18 19 20

8 + 6 = 14
addition sentence

1. 5 + 8

0 1 2 3 4 5 6 7 8 9 10 11 12 13 14 15 16 17 18 19 20

5 + 8 =
addition sentence

2. 4 + 7

0 1 2 3 4 5 6 7 8 9 10 11 12 13 14 15 16 17 18 19 20

4 + 7 =
addition sentence

3. 9 + 4

0 1 2 3 4 5 6 7 8 9 10 11 12 13 14 15 16 17 18 19 20

9 + 4 =
addition sentence

Using a Number Line for Sums Greater Than 10
Worksheet 1

Name _____

Date _____

1. Use rods on the number line to help find the sum.
2. Complete the addition sentence.

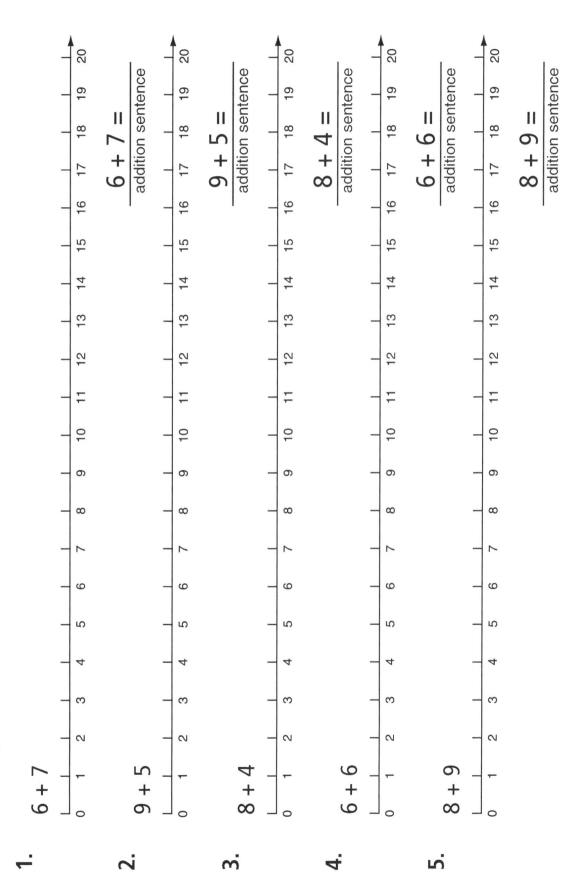

1. 6 + 7

0 1 2 3 4 5 6 7 8 9 10 11 12 13 14 15 16 17 18 19 20

6 + 7 = _____
addition sentence

2. 9 + 5

0 1 2 3 4 5 6 7 8 9 10 11 12 13 14 15 16 17 18 19 20

9 + 5 = _____
addition sentence

3. 8 + 4

0 1 2 3 4 5 6 7 8 9 10 11 12 13 14 15 16 17 18 19 20

8 + 4 = _____
addition sentence

4. 6 + 6

0 1 2 3 4 5 6 7 8 9 10 11 12 13 14 15 16 17 18 19 20

6 + 6 = _____
addition sentence

5. 8 + 9

0 1 2 3 4 5 6 7 8 9 10 11 12 13 14 15 16 17 18 19 20

8 + 9 = _____
addition sentence

Using a Number Line for Sums Greater Than 10
Worksheet 2

Addition & Subtraction with Cuisenaire® Rods   185

Name _____

Date _____

1. Use rods on the number line to find the answers.
2. Write the completed number sentence.

1.

0 1 2 3 4 5 6 7 8 9 10 11 12 13 14 15 16 17 18 19 20

_____ number sentence

2.

0 1 2 3 4 5 6 7 8 9 10 11 12 13 14 15 16 17 18 19 20

_____ number sentence

3.

0 1 2 3 4 5 6 7 8 9 10 11 12 13 14 15 16 17 18 19 20

_____ number sentence

4.

0 1 2 3 4 5 6 7 8 9 10 11 12 13 14 15 16 17 18 19 20

_____ number sentence

5.

0 1 2 3 4 5 6 7 8 9 10 11 12 13 14 15 16 17 18 19 20

_____ number sentence

6.

0 1 2 3 4 5 6 7 8 9 10 11 12 13 14 15 16 17 18 19 20

_____ number sentence

Using a Number Line for Sums Greater Than 10
Master

Name _____

Date _____

1. Make an addition table.
2. Fill in all the sums.
3. Look for patterns in the finished table.

+	1	2	3	4	5	6	7	8	9	10
1										
2										
3										
4										
5										
6										
7										
8										
9										
10										

4. Use rods to check the sums.

Making an Addition Table for Sums Through 20
Worksheet

Addition & Subtraction with Cuisenaire® Rods   187

Name _____

Date _____

1. Find each sum without using rods.

1. 6 + 7 = _____

2. 5 + 9 = _____

3. 8 + 8 = _____

4. 3 + 10 = _____

5. 9 + 8 = _____

6. 7 + 7 = _____

7. 4 + 7 = _____

8. 9 + 6 = _____

9. 8 + 6 = _____

10. 10 + 7 = _____

11. 2 + 9 = _____

12. 4 + 8 = _____

13. 5 + 6 = _____

14. 8 + 7 = _____

15. 8 + 10 = _____

16. 7 + 9 = _____

2. Check your answers using rods on the number line.

0 1 2 3 4 5 6 7 8 9 10 11 12 13 14 15 16 17 18 19 20

Checking Addition Facts Through 20
Worksheet

Name _____

Date _____

1. Color the rod picture for each subtraction story.
2. Find the difference.
3. Write the complete subtraction sentence.

Example:

$$12 - 5 = 7$$

subtraction sentence

1. $18 - 9$

subtraction sentence: _____

2. $13 - 6$

subtraction sentence: _____

3. $20 - 7$

subtraction sentence: _____

4. $14 - 8$

subtraction sentence: _____

Name _____

Date _____

1. Color the rod picture for each subtraction story.
2. Find the difference.
3. Write the complete subtraction sentence.

1. 11 – 5

subtraction sentence: _____

2. 17 – 7

subtraction sentence: _____

3. 14 – 9

subtraction sentence: _____

4. 18 – 2

subtraction sentence: _____

5. 15 – 6

subtraction sentence: _____

Addition & Subtraction with Cuisenaire® Rods

Practicing Subtraction Sentences with Teen Numbers
Worksheet 2

Name _____

Date _____

1. Write a subtraction story starting with a number greater than 10 and less than 20.
2. Color the rod picture for each subtraction story. 3. Find the difference.
4. Write the complete subtraction sentence.

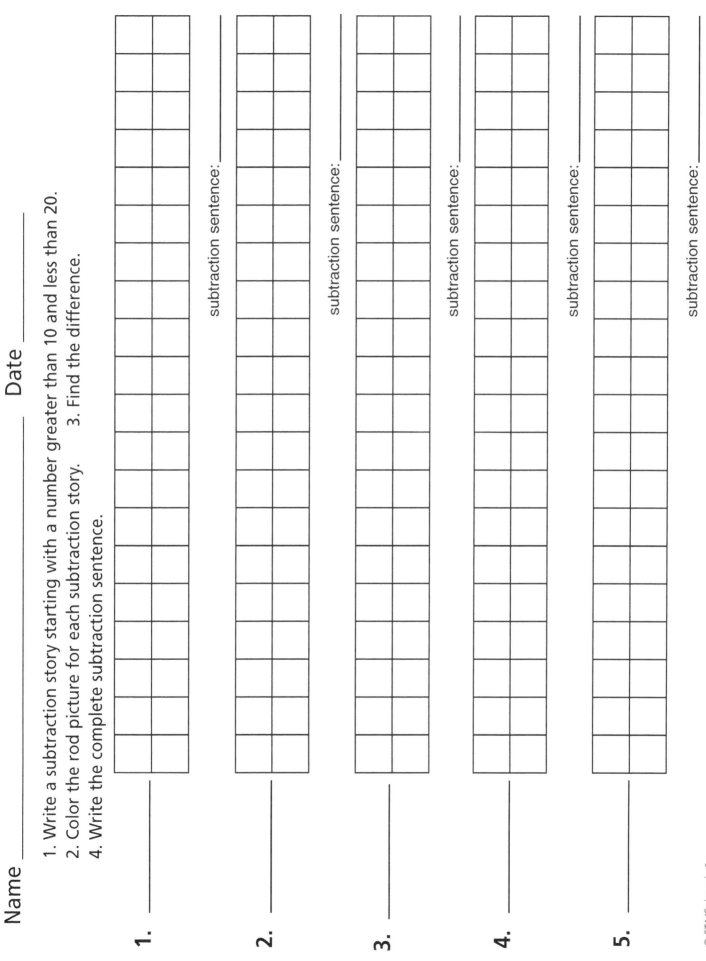

1. _____

subtraction sentence: _____

2. _____

subtraction sentence: _____

3. _____

subtraction sentence: _____

4. _____

subtraction sentence: _____

5. _____

subtraction sentence: _____

Practicing Subtraction Sentences with Teen Numbers
Master

Name _____

Date _____

1. Find each difference without using rods.

1. 14 – 9 = _____

2. 10 – 3 = _____

3. 13 – 7 = _____

4. 16 – 8 = _____

5. 17 – 9 = _____

6. 14 – 7 = _____

7. 11 – 4 = _____

8. 15 – 6 = _____

9. 14 – 8 = _____

10. 17 – 7 = _____

11. 11 – 2 = _____

12. 12 – 8 = _____

13. 15 – 7 = _____

14. 11 – 6 = _____

15. 18 – 10 = _____

16. 16 – 7 = _____

2. Check your answers using rods on the number line.

Checking Subtraction Facts
Worksheet

Name _____

Date _____

1. Find each sum or difference without using rods.

1. 8 + 6 = _____   **2.** 9 − 7 = _____   **3.** 15 − 8 = _____

4. 5 + 9 = _____   **5.** 10 − 4 = _____   **6.** 10 + 4 = _____

7. 7 + 8 = _____   **8.** 4 + 7 = _____   **9.** 12 − 9 = _____

10. 16 − 6 = _____   **11.** 14 − 7 = _____   **12.** 8 + 9 = _____

13. 13 − 8 = _____   **14.** 16 − 9 = _____

2. Check your answers using rods on the number line.

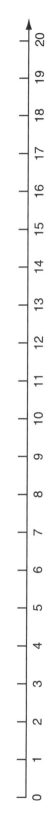

Name _____

1. Find each sum or difference without using rods.

1. 5
      + 4
     _____

2. 9
      − 6
     _____

3. 4
      + 8
     _____

4. 11
      − 9
     _____

5. 8
      + 6
     _____

6. 14
      − 9
     _____

7. 12
      − 5
     _____

8. 4
      + 9
     _____

9. 11
      − 3
     _____

10. 8
       + 8
      _____

11. 16
       − 9
      _____

12. 6
       + 9
      _____

2. Check your answers using rods on the number line.

0 1 2 3 4 5 6 7 8 9 10 11 12 13 14 15 16 17 18 19 20

Name _____ Date _____

1. Find each sum.
2. Use rods or rod pictures to help.

1. 4 + 1 + 5   4 + 1 + 5 = _____

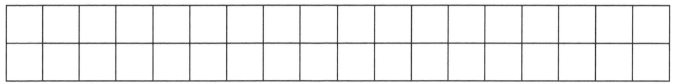

2. 6 + 8 + 2   6 + 8 + 2 = _____

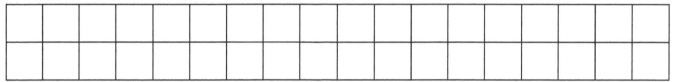

3. 4 + 4 + 6   4 + 4 + 6 = _____

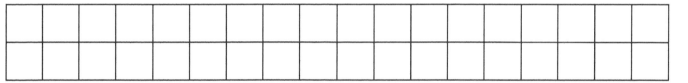

4. 7 + 3 + 5   7 + 3 + 5 = _____

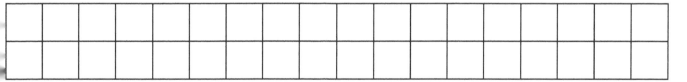

5. 8 + 9 + 1   8 + 9 + 1 = _____

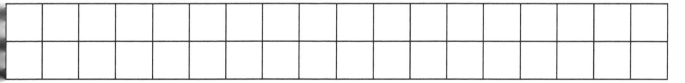

Finding Sums with More Than Two Addends
Worksheet 1

Name _____ Date _____

1. Find each sum.
2. Use rods or rod pictures to help.
3. Write your answers.

1. 2 + 3 + 4 = _____

2. 7 + 8 + 5 = _____

3. 6 + 1 + 2 = _____

4. 6 + 5 + 4 = _____

5. 2 + 7 + 5 = _____

6. 3 + 8 + 4 = _____

7. 5 + 5 + 3 = _____

8. 8 + 2 + 10 = _____

9.
```
    9
    3
  + 1
  ____
```

10.
```
    7
    2
  + 3
  ____
```

11.
```
    6
    5
  + 7
  ____
```

12.
```
    5
    7
  + 5
  ____
```

13.
```
    8
    4
  + 2
  ____
```

14.
```
    1
    8
  + 9
  ____
```

Finding Sums with More Than Two Addends
Worksheet 2

Name _____ Date _____

1. Write the code for the rod that matches each train of white rods.
2. Find the value of each word in terms of white rods.

Example:

10W	4W	9W	8W
O	P	E	N

$$\begin{array}{r} 10 \\ 4 \\ 9 \\ +\ 8 \\ \hline 31 \end{array}$$

Total Value = 31W

1.

6W	9W	8W

Total Value = _____

2.

4W	2W	10W	6W

Total Value = _____

3.

7W	8W	9W	9W

Total Value = _____

4.

9W	6W	3W	9W

Total Value = _____

5.

8W	10W	1W

Total Value = _____

6.

10W	2W	6W	9W	2W

Total Value = _____

Finding the Value of Rod Code Words
Worksheet 1

Name _____ Date _____

1. Write the code for the rod that matches each train of white rods.
2. Find the value of each word in terms of white rods.

1.

4W	9W	8W

Total Value = _____

2.

6W	2W	10W	4W

Total Value = _____

3.

6W	10W	10W	2W

Total Value = _____

4.

7W	8W	9W	1W

Total Value = _____

5.

8W	10W	8W	9W

Total Value = _____

6.

2W	5W	9W

Total Value = _____

7.

7W	8W	10W	1W	8W

Total Value = _____

Finding the Value of Rod Code Words
Worksheet 2

Name _____ Date _____

1. Write the code for the rod that matches each train of white rods.
2. Find the value of each word in terms of white rods.

1.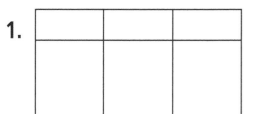

Total Value = _____

2.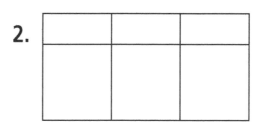

Total Value = _____

3.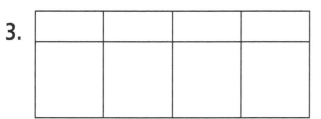

Total Value = _____

4.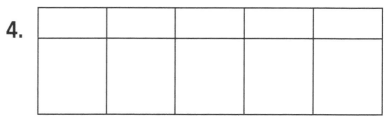

Total Value = _____

5.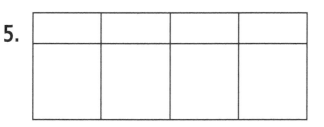

Total Value = _____

6.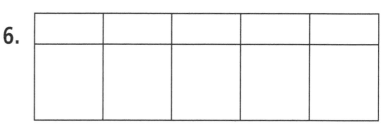

Total Value = _____

7.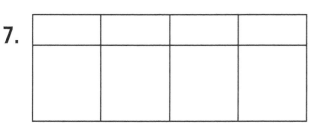

Total Value = _____

8.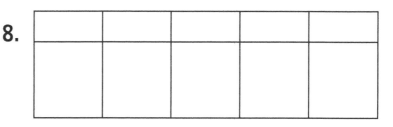

Total Value = _____

Finding the Value of Rod Code Words
Master

© ETA/Cuisenaire®

Name _____ Date _____

1. Cover the design with rods.
2. Find the value of each design in terms of white rods.
3. Write an addition sentence for each design.
4. Cover the design in a different way to check your answer.

Example:

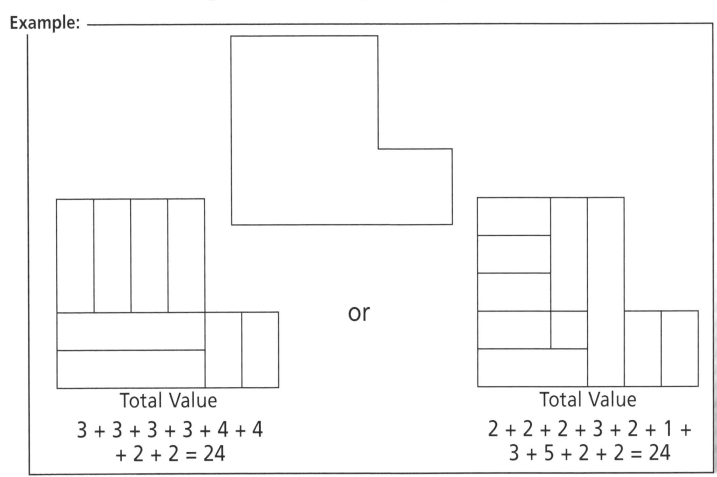

or

Total Value

3 + 3 + 3 + 3 + 4 + 4
+ 2 + 2 = 24

Total Value

2 + 2 + 2 + 3 + 2 + 1 +
3 + 5 + 2 + 2 = 24

1.

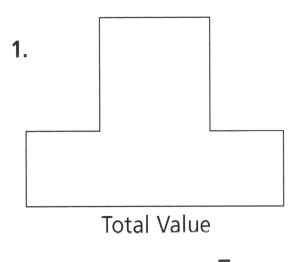

Total Value

_____ = _____

2.

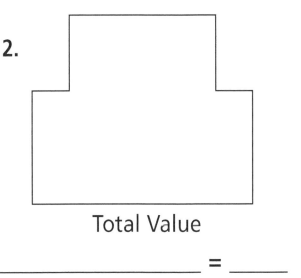

Total Value

_____ = _____

Finding the Value of Rod Designs
Worksheet 1

Name _____ Date _____

1. Cover the design with rods.
2. Find the value of each design in terms of white rods.
3. Write an addition sentence for each design.
4. Cover the design in a different way to check your answer.

1.

Total Value

_____ = _____

2.

Total Value

_____ = _____

3.

Total Value

_____

= _____

4.

Total Value

_____

= _____

Name _____ Date _____

1. You have one rod of each color. What is the total value of the ten rods in terms of white rods? _____

2. You have all the even rods: red, purple, dark green, brown, and orange. What is the total value of the five rods in terms of white rods? _____
_____

3. You have all the odd rods: white, green, yellow, black, and blue. What is the total value of the five rods in terms of white rods? _____
_____

4. Check that your answers to questions 2 and 3 add to your answer to question 1. Why? _____
_____
_____
_____

5. You have five red rods, three green rods, and one purple rod. What is the total value of the nine rods in terms of white rods? _____

6. You have five rods that have a total value of 17 white rods. Four of the rods are white, red, green, and black. What color is the fifth rod? _____
_____

7. You have six rods that have a total value of 30 white rods. Five of the rods are red, green, purple, dark green, and brown. What color is the sixth rod?
_____

Name _____ Date _____

Find the rods that fit the clues.

1. You have two rods. The rods have a sum of 15 and a difference of 3. What are the colors of the two rods? _____   _____

2. You have three rods, all the same color. The rods have a sum of 15. What is the color of the three rods? _____

3. You have two rods. The rods have a sum of 13 and a difference of 5. What are the colors of the two rods? _____   _____

4. You have six rods that are all the same color. The rods have a sum of 12. What is the color of the six rods? _____

5. You have three rods that are all different colors. All three rods are even rods. The rods have a sum of 20. Find two collections of rods that you could have.
   1. _____   _____   _____
   2. _____   _____   _____

6. You have three rods that are all different colors. The rods have a sum of 15. Find four different collections of rods that you could have.
   1. _____   _____   _____
   2. _____   _____   _____
   3. _____   _____   _____
   4. _____   _____   _____

7. You have four rods that are all different colors. The rods have a sum of 18. Find four possible collections of rods that you could have.
   1. _____   _____   _____   _____
   2. _____   _____   _____   _____
   3. _____   _____   _____   _____
   4. _____   _____   _____   _____

Name _____ Date _____

1. Read the clue.
2. Find the correct rod code word.
3. Then find the total value of each rod code word in terms of white rods.

Total
Value

1. color of a plant __G__ ____ ____ ____ ____   _____

2. body part used for seeing ____ ____ __E__   _____

3. a part of your leg __K__ ____ ____ ____   _____

4. used for writing ____ __E__ ____   _____

5. cowboy games __R__ ____ ____ ____ ____   _____

6. color of an apple ____ ____ __D__   _____

7. small body of water __P__ ____ ____ ____   _____

8. period of seven days ____ ____ ____ __K__   _____

9. state in the U.S. ____ __E__ ____ __Y__ ____ ____ ____   _____

10. breakfast food __E__ ____ ____   _____

11. not wet ____ __R__ ____   _____

12. fancy dress __G__ ____ ____ ____   _____

Solving Rod Word Problems
Worksheet 3

© ETA/Cuisenaire®

NOTES

NOTES

NOTES

NOTES